William Everson:
The Light The Shadow Casts

– A Stride Conversation Piece –

Other Stride Conversation Pieces:

The Cool Eye
Lawrence Ferlinghettit talks to Alexis Lykiard

Emotional Geology: the writings of Brian Louis Pearce
edited by Rupert M. Loydell

Chasing The Vibration: Meetings With Creative Musicians
by Graham Lock (with photos by Nick White)

At The Heart Of Things: the poetry and prose of David Miller
Andrew Bick, Guy Birchard, James Crouch, Robert G. Hampson,
Robert Sheppard, with David Miller

Mixtery: a festschrift for Anthony Braxton
edited by Graham Lock

WILLIAM EVERSON:
THE LIGHT THE SHADOW CASTS

Five interviews with William Everson
plus corresponding poems

edited and introduced by

Clifton Ross

WILLIAM EVERSON:
THE LIGHT THE SHADOW CASTS
First edition 1996
Interviews & editing © Clifton Ross
Poems © estate William Everson
All rights reserved

ISBN 1 873012 95 0 (UK)

ISBN 915117-05-3 (USA)

Cover photo of William Everson
by David Fetcho © 1994
Cover design Joe Pieczenko

A Stride Conversation Piece
published in the USA by
New Earth Publications
1921 Ashby Avenue
Berkeley, CA 94703

and in Europe by
Stride Publications
11 Sylvan Road, Exeter
Devon EX4 6EW
England

Contents

WILLIAM EVERSON: THE LIGHT THE SHADOW CASTS

Introduction: William Everson: The Splendor in the Shadow *7*
Poem: The Roots of Arousal *19*

First Interview: Sacramentalism, Totemism and Astrology *21*
Poem: A Canticle to the Christ in the Holy Eucharist *30*

Second Interview: Vocation, Witness and Encounter *33*
Poem: A Canticle to the Waterbirds *44*

Third Interview: The Poet and the Prophet *47*
Poem: Who is She That Looketh Forth as the Morning *69*

Fourth Interview: The Engendering Flood *73*
Poem: The Blood of the Poet *86*

Fifth Interview: The Poet and the World *89*

POEMS OF THE PSYCHOID CHRIST

Dark God of Eros *102*
The Song the Body Dreamed in the Spirit's Mad Behest *104*
God Germed in Raw Granite *106*
The Word *108*
In Savage Wastes *109*
In All these Acts *116*

Epilogue: by William Everson *119*

The need of his times works inside the artist without his wanting it, seeing it, or understanding its true significance. In this sense he is close to the seer, the prophet, the mystic. And it is precisely when he does not represent the existing canon but transforms and overturns it that his function rises to the level of the sacral, for he then gives utterance to the authentic and direct revelation of the *numinosum.*

     – Erich Neumann, *Art And The Creative Unconscious*

Introduction
William Everson: The Light in the Shadow

The poetry of William Everson is as much a product of the rich alluvial earth of California as the gold and grapes that brought the state its fame. It is as intricate and diverse as the culture of his native land, as the culture of which he is an essential ingredient. Those familiar with Everson's work are unreserved in their praise of him. Saying that T.S. Eliot was the greatest religious poet to write in English in the first half of the century, Albert Gelpi went on in his 'Afterword' to *The Veritable Years, 1949-1966* (1978, Black Sparrow Press) to proclaim William Everson "the most important religious poet of the second half of the century". Poet William Stafford attributes much of the campus radicalism of the 1960s to Everson's conscientious objection in World War Two and describes him as "one of the most notable, extreme, jagged figures of modern American poetry" (*The Achievement of Brother Antoninus*, 1967, Scott Foresman and Co.). The author of over forty books, Everson's descriptive bibliography (*William Everson: A Descriptive Bibliography, 1934-1976*, 1977 Scarecrow Press, Inc.) is itself over one hundred pages long. His contribution to North American poetry has been invaluable and his contributions to Jungian psychology and theology have yet to be fully appreciated.

Nevertheless, Everson is still little known on the east coast of the United States and this book is his first to be published in the United Kingdom. The reason for this is that he is primarily a regional poet. He writes in, of and for California. This does not mean that the themes of his poetry lack universality, but that the particular landscape and language of the poems reflect the poets environment.

Connected with this is his vocal opposition to Modernism. Modernism, in true classical mode, denigrates regionalism in its search for a universal aesthetic. As Everson himself put it in the introduction to *Archetype West: The Pacific Coast As A Literary Region*: "Of course, regionalism has had a bad press since the advent of the Modernist movement early in this century. That movement was international in its outlook and regarded the regional accent as provincial and myopic, emphasizing content at the expense of quality and hence constituting a threat to both culture and art. Over against this perspective I believe that the impress of place on man's artifacts is something not only authentic but absolutely ineradicable…"

To Everson's critique of Modernism might be added the words of Otto Rank, who said that, in Modernism, the "compelling motive is *fear of life* and experience" (emphasis his). It would indeed be difficult to find any common traits between the exuberant, celebratory Everson and the Prufrockian Modernist (or for that matter, Postmodernist): They are poles apart. Everson's entire life has been predicated on the romantic thirst for experience and whole-hearted embracing of the life process. Modernism has stood for objectivity while Everson, along with the existentialists, personalists and other rebels of this century, have maintained the primacy of subjectivity. Language poetry, concrete poetry and other solipsistic manifestations of the remnants of Modernism and post-Modernism all indicate a cultural dead end which is not true of regionalist work.

While Everson's fame may have been limited earlier this century as a result of his unpopular resistance to Modernism, this promises to change as that movement whimpers to its death in the aridity of post-Modernism. Everson will point out that with the advent of Einstein's theory of relativity and the paradigm shift toward the holistic view of Eastern mysticism, the fragmented, mechanistic worldview of Modernism was already passé at its inception. With the renewed interest in nature over the past twenty years, as well as the growing awareness of California as a cultural center in its own right, Everson is sure to be affirmed by this and future generations as one of America's greatest voices in poetry.

•

The first interviews printed in this volume took place in January of 1980 at William Everson's house near Davenport, California in an area Everson calls "Kingfisher Flat". At the time I was a young poet who had encountered Everson's work in Chad Walsh's anthology, *Today's Poets,* several years earlier while living in rural Oklahoma. I still remember the awe and admiration I felt when I first read 'Hospice of the Word' about the Peter Maurin Catholic Worker House with the strong images of the "grimed sink" and dingy surroundings where Everson had gone to encounter Christ. There was something real in those lines, something of flesh, blood and bone, unlike the disembodied god of the devotional or religious poetry with which I had become familiar since my own conversion to Christianity during the Jesus Movement of the early 1970's.

Unconsciously, what I responded to was Everson's earthy, peasant sensibility rooted in the San Joaquin Valley of California. Modestly hoping to be the Valley's "poet laureate", the first period of his life, formed in the shadow of his master, Robinson Jeffers, was idyllic. His pantheism reflected Everson's profound connection to nature, the earth and the life of farm work. But this world was shattered by World War II when Everson made the decision to resist the draft. As a result of this stand Everson was sent to the Waldport, Oregon work camp for conscientious objectors, where he became the director of the National Fine Arts program for C.O.s. At Waldport he encountered other radical artists, musicians, printers and writers including Brodus Erle, Clayton James, Kemper Nomland, William Eshelman, Adrian Wilson and Morris Graves.

Everson returned to California in 1946 and moved to the Bay Area where he became a central figure in the San Francisco Literary Renaissance which included such poetic giants as Kenneth Rexroth, Robert Duncan, Jack Spicer and others. Of this period we have *The Residual Years*, a fine collection of poetry published by New Directions in New York and introduced by Kenneth Rexroth, Everson's mentor.

Not only did the San Francisco Renaissance represent a new force in poetry, but it also took up the struggle for renewal in politics, society and religion. Anarchist study groups, led by Kenneth Rexroth and attended by the literary luminaries of the time (including Everson), drew outcasts and malcontents from all over the United States. These meetings had a powerful impact on an emerging generation of writers that would later form the "Beat" movement, including Lawrence Ferlinghetti, Gary Snyder, Allen Ginsberg and others. Rexroth's anarchist Buddhism provided the spiritual inspiration for this disillusioned "beats" who'd found nothing either in the insipid optimism of post-World-War-Two America or in the only viable alternative at the time, the rigid ideology of Communism then under attack by Joseph McCarthy. In contrast to all other movements of the time, the Renaissance was a lively alternative, even if numerically insignificant.

Everson once said (interview in the Fall/Spring 1978-1979 issue of *Imprint: Oregon*) that the "whole San Francisco Renaissance had in some way a powerful inception at Waldport" and this "Waldport movement was the nucleus of the San Francisco Renaissance". According to Rexroth "William Everson. . . is probably the most profoundly moving and durable of the poets of the San Francisco Renaissance".

The effect the San Francisco Renaissance had on North American culture was phenomenal. As Kierkegaard says in *Either/Or*: "Tremendous and powerful causes sometimes produce small and unimpressive effects, sometimes none at all; then again it happens that a brisk little cause produces a colossal effect." The "colossal effect" from the "brisk little cause" of the Renaissance, in this case, was the Beat movement and the counter-cultural revolution of the 1960's.

Everson's conversion to Catholicism may be seen as an unconscious attempt to find his balance, having, at that juncture, exhausted the possibilities offered by his pantheist anarchism. This search for balance took him out of the Dionysian, anarchist, bohemian environment and into the rigidly structured institution of the pre-Vatican II Roman Catholic Church. Psychologically, this was Everson's attempt to resolve the masculine, paternal dimension of his personality, especially after the unexpected death of his father while Everson was interned for "refusing to wear the symbols of the patriarchy". Everson thus disappeared from the bohemian scene for a number of years, retiring into the monastic life where he began his study of Christian theology and Jungian psychology.

Nevertheless, as Thomas Merton says, one goes into the desert not to escape the voices of the world, but "in order to hear those voices more clearly". Outside the walls of the monastery Everson's younger comrades in poetry, particularly Allen Ginsberg, were flashing their newly discovered sexuality at all of repressed America. By contrast with the members of the Renaissance who quietly crafted their poems and discussed subversive ideas in subdued tones, the Beats shouted their outrage. Ginsberg's statements in *Howl* and *America* ("America go fuck your bombs") could no doubt be heard behind the monastery walls and Everson, now going by his religious name of Brother Antoninus, felt compelled to respond. His focus on psychology and mysticism had already led him to develop an erotic mysticism all his own and now he pulled his ideas together in what would turn out to be his signature poem, 'River-Root, A Syzygy'.

This poem, over a thousand lines long, is an orgiastic celebration of the poet's own conception through the imagined love-making of his parents. The poem works out Jungian polarities and evolves climactically with astounding power. In fact, Brother Antoninus kept this poem from the view of his superiors at the time it was written and, as a result, it was nearly twenty years before it was printed. Today it stands as a masterpiece of Anglo-American poetry and a tribute to the genius formed out of the cauldron of the San Francisco Renaissance.

In addition to 'River-Root', Brother Antoninus concentrated his energies while in the Dominican Order on expounding an erotic mysticism a la St. John of the Cross in books like *The Crooked Lines Of God*, *The Hazards Of Holiness*, *The Rose Of Solitude*, *The Mate Flight Of Eagles* and *The Poet Is Dead*, his memorial to Robinson Jeffers, all collected in *The Veritable Years*. Such writing in North American Roman Catholicism in the 1950's caused no small ripple and more than once Brother Antoninus had to defend his work before his superiors.

In 1969, at a poetry reading at the University of California in Davis, Antoninus dramatically stripped off his clerical robe and left the Order to marry Susanna Rickson, a young runaway woman he'd been counseling. For the next few years the poet, now William Everson once again, worked to integrate his poetry, philosophy and theology and make meaning out of the crooked lines of his life.

Immediately after leaving the Order the Eversons moved to Stinson Beach, the setting for *Man-Fate*. They later moved to Davenport, ten miles north of Santa Cruz, touching home at last at Kingfisher Flat with *The Masks Of Drought*. An internationally recognized printer, Everson began teaching poetry and hand-press printing at the University of California, Santa Cruz. Within a few years, however, he developed Parkinson's disease and soon retired from teaching to devote himself full time to his writing. At the time of his death in June, 1994, he was completing *The Integral Years* (which will include *Man-*

Fate, The Masks Of Drought and uncollected poems) and launching into an autobiographical epic work entitled 'The Engendering Flood'.

•

I first heard William Everson read at Cody's Bookstore, Berkeley, in late 1978. Everson was accompanied that night by a younger Dominican, a priest named William Ruddy, whose powerful poems were driven by the syncopated rhythms of India where he'd lived and worked for a number of years. The younger poet's reading was impressive but Everson was not to be outshone. His warm familiarity and ease was balanced by a strong tension as he "built on silence", stalking his audience as he paced back and forth and stared down the breathless crowd. Part of his technique involved talking slowly and thoughtfully about mundane events and then turning to a poem by which he grabbed the listening audience with what Everson called "the giant hand" of the work itself.

I met Ruddy in Moe's Bookstore several weeks later and, after a long conversation in one of the aisles he gave me a ride home to my apartment in Oakland where we continued the conversation until late in the evening. We began a long friendship that night which involved him in our monthly writer's groups that had formed out of the Christian community to which I belonged and soon I began organizing monthly or bimonthly public poetry readings with Ruddy and other community poets. The peak moment of this period came in August of 1979 when we arranged a reading with William Everson at what I billed, in poetically grandiose terms, the "Third Epoch Poetry Reading".

Several of us went down to Davenport to pick up Bill from his house at Kingfisher Flat. On the way back to Berkeley I explained a bit of Nicholas Berdyaev's ideas and their connection to what some of us were doing in the Berkeley Christian community. At the reading itself I read a passage from Berdyaev's *The Meaning Of The Creative Act* to the audience of sixty or more who'd gathered for the event. Having successfully conveyed my enthusiasm for Berdyaev I gave Bill some copies of the Russian thinker's books. Everson and I began a correspondence that centered primarily on Berdyaev and who later became the focus of several interviews printed here.

Nicholas Berdyaev was a Russian Orthodox philosopher and mystic who has been called, with some degree of justification, a gnostic existentialist. He proposed creativity as the highest spiritual path and humanity's chief end. God, Berdyaev believed, could not be found in any orthodoxy or sacrament but only through the creative act. In creation the human enters divinity and is united with it. "Through [humanity's] creativeness God in the world is finally revealed." To the western Christian this might sound heterodox but in fact it echoes a phrase of St. Ireneus (and later restated by St. Athanasius and others), one of the earliest Fathers of the Christian Church, who proclaimed that "God became a person so that the person might become god". The Eastern Orthodox church has always professed a belief in the idea of "theosis" or divinization wherein the believer attains to godhood by means of faith in Christ, the Human God.

Partaking in this divine nature of the Creator, Berdyaev believed that the only appropriate human response was to create. "What God expects from humanity," says Berdyaev in *Truth And Revelation* (p.119), "is not servile submission, not obedience, not the fear of condemnation, but free creative acts. But this was hidden until the appointed time. The revelation which is concerned with this cannot be divine only, it must be a divine-human revelation in which [the person] takes an active and creative part."

Berdyaev, using the mythic frame of Joachim di Fiores, also conceived of history in terms of three epochs. The first epoch was governed by the wrathful Yahweh, the god of the Law, in the epoch of the Father. The second epoch was the epoch of Redemption, imaged in Jesus, the Son. The third and final epoch in Berdyaev's scheme was the epoch of creativity, the epoch of the Spirit. In this Trinitarian conception of history Berdyaev located modern humanity on the verge of the new age of creativity when humanity would be divinized though the creative act in harmony with God by the Holy Spirit.

Nicolas Berdyaev was an intuitive, mystical thinker, a true existentialist. He engaged in what Robert Bly might have called "leaping" philosophy, although this is not to say that his writing lacked unity or purpose. Indeed, as Everson himself once mentioned to me, Berdyaev's first important book, *The Meaning Of The Creative Act*, seemed to have been written in a single breath, almost without paragraph breaks.

While Berdyaev's writings dealt primarily with philosophy, he could never be accused of living in an ivory tower. In over thirty books, Berdyaev spoke the truth as he saw it without regard for the consequences. Suffering exile for his part in the 1905 Revolution against the Tsar, Berdyaev was later nearly executed by the Orthodox hierarchy for his defense of heretic monks and their right to dissent, being saved only by the sudden explosion of the Russian Revolution. Solzhenitsyn describes in the third chapter of *The Gulag Archipelago* how Berdyaev before his Communist interrogators not only didn't deny his ideas but made a forceful presentation of them. Exiled again under the Communists for his Christian personalism, Berdyaev finally died in Paris after having devoted himself for years to a tireless attack on both communism and capitalism while advocating what he called "personalist socialism".

The interest Everson took in Berdyaev was natural, based on his profound and passionate respect for personality and the individual. This natural personalism had found institutional affirmation in the Catholic Worker movement which Everson joined briefly after his conversion to Catholicism and prior to his entering the Dominicans. The Catholic Worker, an anarchist movement founded by Dorothy Day and Peter Maurin, was philosophically inspired by Nicholas

Berdyaev, as William D. Miller points out in his introduction to his history of the Catholic Worker Movement, *A Harsh And Dreadful Love* (1974, Doubleday Image). This movement would have had an obvious appeal to Everson after his conversion, especially given his pantheist anarchist values.

Everson, in *Man-Fate*, had struggled with his identity and sought a way of uniting these three distinct periods of his life. Through Berdyaev's cosmology Everson was introduced to a model by which he could at last pull these three periods of his life together in the poet's religion of creativity. Following Joachim di Fiore's Trinitarian conception of history as reinterpreted by Berdyaev, Everson at once recognized how these three historical epochs bore a resemblance to his own life story. The first epoch of his life was the period of his Jeffersian pantheism, his youthful anarchist phase. In the second epoch of Everson's life he attained redemption through his conversion to Christ and entered the Dominican Order, passing through his institutional period, symbolized by his embrace of the patriarchy he'd earlier rejected. The third epoch was that of Spirit and creativity, the epoch of freedom from the institution and the deep mystery of the divine in the human. This final epoch was represented by Everson's departure from the institution of the Dominican Order when he took on the role of the shaman and encountered Christ at the level of the psychoid.

•

Everson would describe himself as a "mystic of the flesh", as he does in the third interview printed here. As a result, his aesthetic and theology moves in a direction contrary to traditional Roman Catholic theology as personified by two theologians he mentions by name (in the second interview printed here), Jacques Maritain and Thomas Merton who, while intellectually affirming the erotic, still look upwards to heaven or the "higher" regions of the intellect or spirit for the light of God. By nature, Everson's focus has always been turned toward the root forces of creation, the base energies of the body, tapping into the sexual, the erotic, the "psychoid" levels beneath even the unconscious.

It was Jim Neafsey, one of the participants in that third interview, who first noted Everson's unique connection to the psychoid realm of consciousness and, fortunately, pursued a line of questions that revealed the hidden dimensions of the poet's aesthetic. Combining the tradition of ancient healers, poets and seers known as shaman (see M. Eliade's book, *Shamanism*) with a Jungian understanding of human consciousness, Everson has developed an original and highly compelling theory of creativity and spirituality. Traditionally, the shaman descends into the unconscious of his/her patient in order to ascertain the nature of a given illness. The deepest level of the unconscious, which is almost no longer consciousness per se, was labeled the *psychoid* by Carl Jung. For Everson, this synthesis of the third epoch is a level of human development in consciousness rather than in time and is not an elevation out of the world into "cosmic consciousness" but rather a deepening of our connection with the earth and the material plane of life. It is therefore to the nether regions, to the dark world of the unconscious, that he points us for an encounter with Christ.

In a sense, then, the Psychoid Christ is the shadow side of the Cosmic Christ as celebrated by the theologian Matthew Fox. While the Cosmic Christ is encountered in the upper chakras, as it were, in the sublime regions of the clouds with angels, the Psychoid Christ is found at the base of the spine reaching into the primal forces of the earth like a coiled serpent. This theological emphasis relates to Everson's avowed attempt to get back in touch with the "aboriginal forces of life on this continent" before the Conquest. And so in Everson's poem 'In All These Acts' the poet's Christ "crouches and seethes" and is revealed in the acts of violence wherein he is

...pitched forward on the crucifying stroke,
juvescent, that will spring Him
Out of the germ, out of the belly of the dying buck,
Out of the father-phallus and the torn-up root.

Christ is equated with the Dark God of Eros, a "stone-channeled beast of ecstasy and fire,/ The angelic wisdom in the serpentine desire". This imagery refers us to the indigenous Christ-figure of Central America, Quetzalcoatl, the plumed serpent. Quetzalcoatl, very likely a historical figure who brought high culture and spirituality to the Mayans and decried human sacrifice, in mythic terms is an image of the human person: the spinal column that stands erect with the angelic organs of tongue and labia, organs of speech or verbal creation above, while below, at the base, are the "serpentine" organs (also tongue or labia, depending on sex) of physical creation, procreation:"As above, so below."

Yet everything else also directs Everson downward and into his origins: his origins as a farmer who loves the earth; his origins as a working person, his erotic vitality and earthy wisdom that arises from these beginnings. As a Jungian Everson would maintain that the conscious mind arises out of the unconscious. As a Christian Everson would maintain the necessity of the Incarnation, the descent of God into flesh for the ascent of humanity into Godhead. As Jesus overturned the tables of tradition at the temple in the name of the Spirit of Truth, so Everson overturns the exalted idealism of traditional Christian theology with the erotic thrust of his carnal mysticism to reveal the hidden dimension of Christ's personality, His human complexion.

Everson's theology has a resonance with both Wiccan paganism and Kundalini yoga. In Wiccan religion the female deity (Shakti) is also identified with the lowest chakra and the aim of kundalini and tantric yoga is to bring her energy into union with the male deity, Shiva, located in the third eye at the top of the skull. Mircea Eliade describes this process in his book, *Patanjali And Yoga* (1975, Schocken Books): "Absolute reality, the *Urgrund*, contains in itself all dualities and polarities, reunited, reincorporated in a state of absolute unity (*advava*). The Creation and the process of becoming that derives from it represent the explosion of the primordial unity and the separation of the two principles (Shiva-Shakti, etc.)... The goal of Tantrist *sadhana* (practice) is the reunion of the two polar principles in the disciple's soul and body." (p.118)

As Ira Progoff points out in his book, *Jung, Synchronicity And Human Destiny*, Jung conceived of four levels of human cognition: "At the surface is Ego Consciousness. The Personal Unconscious is just below it. Beneath that, extending for a considerable depth, is the transpersonal level of the Collective Unconscious. And at the base is the Psychoid level, reaching into the realm of nature itself." (p. 113) This psychoid level, Progoff tells us, is the "level of existence that is not yet sufficiently advanced for separation and distinctness to be necessary. The psychoid state is thus very much like the Self conceived as cosmos or as a primal chaos. It would in fact be correct to say that the psychoid level of development corresponds in the microcosm to the primal chaos in the universe." (p. 80-81)

This level of human cognition is the plane where nature and humanity interface, a level that Jung himself said was synonymous with the "spiritual". Progoff goes on to say that here, "the manifestation of the macrocosm in the microcosm means that something of the world's divinity has been individualized. When a personality experiences this and participates in it, the experience serves as a link between the human being and God."

Since this level of cognition is "irrepresentable" by definition, the microcosmic equivalent of the cosmic Urgrund (or "original ground of being"), where "the distinct aspects of the psyche have not yet been separated from one another, as archetype and instinct, body and mind...", this is the level of immediate and direct encounter with the Universe.

For this reason Everson emphasizes the root energies of creation (the erotic) as the point of spiritual encounter rather than the upper, supra-rational regions of the intellect, in the Ego Consciousness or the crown chakra. And it is this particular focus as a theologian, his approach to God as a descent, that distinguishes Everson from most theologians of this century.

Matthew Fox's theology would theoretically affirm this emphasis on a Psychoid Christ, yet there is a basic difference between Everson's conception of Christ and Fox's Cosmic Christ. Fox, despite an emphasis on creation and an acknowledgement of the erotic, still encounters Christ at the "upper" levels of consciousness rather than the lower. The Cosmic Christ is still an image of a God-Over-Us rather than the God within or among us. The Cosmic Christ is still envisioned within the framework of traditional Jewish and Christian theology with One God above and one soul in each person. Western civilization is based on this paradigm and reveals in its development both the strengths and weaknesses of this view. While this conception strengthens individuality and is conducive to the creation of adventurous, independent and creative persons of genius, it also tends toward alienation and a sense of isolation. If we each have individual souls, how are we connected? Furthermore, this view tends toward nationalism (as in the case of Zionist Judaism or American Fundamentalism) since the One God can be construed as the Progenitor of the One Mighty Nation.

By contrast, Everson reaches into the darkness, into the Shadow of consciousness, to find the light of God, which the reason Albert Gelpi has said that "Everson's achievement springs... from the Dionysian character of his Christianity". From the "God-Over-Us" Everson takes us to the "God-Beneath-Us", the Urgrund, the Deity that unites us at the deepest level of the psyche. Everson calls us back to the image of the Vine and the branches for a symbol of the Divine-human relationship. His is a chthonic religion, a faith that follows Christ into the underworld in search of spiritual encounter rather than ascending into heaven with the theologians in their search for God. The way, of course, is fraught with dangers of demons lurking in that murky world of shadow but, in Everson's view, this is precisely the calling of the prophet and the artist if either is to attain authenticity in their vocation.

It is not uncommon for poets, that rare breed Ezra Pound called "the antenna of the race", to be attuned to frequencies beyond the pale of normal human hearing. If anything, that is a quality we have come to expect of the artist. Frequently this gift becomes a curse and is paid for with their sanity, their sobriety, or their lives. The integrity between art and life has often been lacking and so the modern age has produced a crop of lopsided geniuses with lives characterized by excess and destruction but who have produced art of exquisite beauty. Only rarely is humanity privileged with a visit from a great artist who has attempted to maintain the integrity between life and art, holiness and creative genius. William Everson lived out his life with exactly that integrity in mind. To the degree to which he has succeeded in that undertaking he has left a legacy to future generations of poets that the way of God and the way of art can be one and the same.

•

Just three months after finishing the final revisions on this book William Everson died in his home at Kingfisher Flat, Davenport, California. Looking over the interviews I am suddenly struck by the great silences he left us, the mysteries to which he referred but which he refused, in his wisdom, to explain, knowing, as any great poet knows, that some things cannot be expressed in human language. The questions reiterated throughout this book, raised by Everson's equation of the poet and the prophet; his fascination with the psychoid and all it implies aesthetically, psychologically and spiritually; the torments and ecstasies of his soul which characterize the shamanic vocation, these mysteries survive him. Certainly Lee Bartlett has done an excellent job of clarifying the reasons behind Everson's dramatic life in his biography *William Everson: The Life of Brother Antonius* (1988, New Directions Books), but the *meaning* of that life can only be found in the work the poet left the world. The grief Bill left us was the passing of his uniquely compelling life, but the joy he left us was his poetry, through which we, and future generations, will be able to celebrate the life of a man in God.

•

Acknowledgements: I'd like to thank Walt Hearn and the editors of *Radix Magazine* who edited and printed portions of an interview in their May 1980 poetry issue. One interview printed here first appeared in *Poetry Flash*. Many thanks to Steve Sibley for his work, ideas, energy and hospitality as this book came together. Also thanks to Elizabeth Hays-Lohrey whose Volkswagen gave up its life getting me down to see Everson for one of these interviews. My gratitude to Bernard Marszalek, Jim Neafsey, Dina Redman, Steve Hays-Lohrey and Steven Herrmann for encouragement, criticism and ideas and thanks to all those, named and unnamed who were silent – or not so silent – participants in these interviews.

Clifton Ross

THE ROOTS OF AROUSAL

England, gaunt raiders up from the narrow sea;
In the dark of the ridges,
Broken under the waves of conquest,
The shattered tribes;
Those gazers out of the stricken eyes,
Under the spell of that moody country,
Shaping the sounds: from the ruinous mouths
The core of existence caught on the tongue,
And the words fashioned.

They are lost in the years of that unknown time,
But the single rhythm of the ancient blood
Remembers the anguish, the hate and desire;
The lips shape a word, and it breaks into being
Struck by the wind of ten thousand years .

And I, not English, in a level valley of the last great west,
Watch from a room in the solstice weather,
And feel back of me trial and error,
The blunt sounds forming,
The importunate utterance of millions of men
Surge up for my ears,
The shape and color of all their awareness
Sung for my mind in the gust of their words.

A poem is alive, we take it with wonder,
Hardly aware of the roots of compulsion
Quickening the timbre of native sounds;
The ancient passion called up to being,
Slow and intense,
Haunting the rhythms of those spoken words.

First Interview
Sacramentalism, Totemism and Astrology

These first two interviews took place over a weekend in January 1980 in Everson's house at Kingfisher Flat. I'd driven as far as Half Moon Bay where the car I'd borrowed blew an engine. Convinced that the "show must go on", I hitchhiked the final thirty or so miles, arriving late afternoon with a large bottle of Oxenblut wine and my primitive recording equipment. The second interview was first published in *Radix Magazine*, May, 1980

.

William Everson: In terms of the Berdyaev I can see that I've been weaned from my own sacramental dependence, my dependence on the sacraments. I hadn't reflected deeply enough on how much externality was involved in my dependence on the sacraments. I was looking at the innards of it. It's kind of like the problem with your mother. You have the problem of the warmth, the maternal warmth and the nurturing of the mother. At the same time there's a spiritual bond in there, too. In some way you have to be weaned away from the mother, weaned away from the breast in order to become a man in the physical sense. So, too, in the spiritual sense I had to be weaned. When I entered the Church the great thing about it was the return to the Mother. The warmth and stability of that sacramental life was to me the great sustaining factor of it throughout. It was so tangible, so concrete, so sensuous. You look at a poem like 'Canticle to the Christ in the Holy Eucharist', the Mount Tamalpais poem where it's just the doe and the buck and the breast and the yoni all merged together What Berdyaev has done for me is... he's shown me the principle of a new interiority that's not so dependent on the external sacraments for its adhesion. I don't know how I'm going to take that in my poetry because I always deal with the concrete and I haven't yet found the key to the inner objectification. That's a strange way to put it because Berdyaev is so opposed to objectification, but if you're going to write about it there has to be some mode of objectification, some way of transference from the external sacraments, which I've been "out of" for ten years, into the new dimension which is just being born within me because of Berdyaev. But I don't have the image for it yet.

Clifton Ross: *Hasn't that image already appeared in* The High Embrace? The nature poems...

Yeah, the nature poems. I mean, there's something almost gothic and churchlike in the description of the High Embrace, something like bringing the Church into nature...

Good question. But what I'm wondering is, well, so much of my sacramental imagery is based on natural phenomena anyhow, even in my most monastic period, like I mentioned on the Tamalpais poem with the deer, the redwoods and all... This is part of the problem. My return to nature after leaving the [Dominican] Order was in some way a return to another breast, to the original breast. There was the mother's breast, then there was Nature when I was a pantheist, then there was the Church. There was Christ, but that was in the natural context. There were the sacraments but I gave them a natural context in most of my writing. In fact I often justified my conversion to the Church by saying it gave me a God I could eat. I could put it in physical terms, which was a sacramental way. That was the source of the power of the poetry, it really was.

And now, if this perspective is going to develop I'm going to have to find a series of metaphors... which relate the X factor, the Unknown, to the appetitive mode. Whether it's a spiritual or a physical appetite it has to have its symbolic correlate if it's going to be effective. And we know, if it's going to work in poetry it's going to have to have the language. And maybe that can be denied, too. Maybe the sacramental language... Maybe the language is a sacrament which I've always held to. I've never thought of that before till this moment but I can see that a good deal of the power of my poetry has been that I would relate to language as sacrament. Maybe not the power of it but at least the urgency of it, the movement of it. Maybe not the ultimate power of it, no, but the movement of it has been. I've always considered language as fundamentally a sacrament, and it's this sacramental quality that I've been able to invest in the language that has been the source or motivating power of my religious poetry. And I'll say that flatly. I've never been able to say it before but that's the truth.

Coming out of an Anabaptist protestant tradition I'm not sure I understand what you, as a Catholic, would mean by sacrament...

Sacrament has to do with the concrete or physical sign signifying a mystery. There's an existential definition of it: "A sign which effects what it signifies..." But to get back to the point, the sacred, that sense of awe, the capacity to invest brute language with a sense of the sacred, the numinous, has been the central characteristic and power of my poetry from the beginning. It was because of the sacramental sense. There's a break-in plane in my verse between *The Residual Years* and *The Veritable Years* and it happened overnight, or in just a few days. Suddenly I'm in another world and that world is a sacramental world. Nature becomes sacramental. In a way it's been like that with the pantheist, with Jeffers. In some ways he's an anti-sacramentalist but that's only because he's transferred it from the Eucharist to the Universe. I transferred it back from the Universe to the Eucharist. I reverse his direction because he began as a Christian and I end as one.

In your last letter you mentioned that Berdyaev had provided you with a basis for your earlier pantheism. You said (in a letter dated the 24th of December) "This morning beginning Chapter 2 (Vallon's biography of Nicholas Berdyaev, Apostle of Freedom, *1960, Philosophical Library, NY), I find the synopsis of the Roman, Protestant and Orthodox views of man intriguing. Practically it doesn't make much difference, since the Redemption in all three views was more than sufficient to overcome the implications of the Fall. I find the Roman valid because it emphasizes our bond with animal life, but what excites me about Berdyaev's Orthodox view is that it ties in with my early pantheism, I mean it provides a Christian base for my pantheistic intuitions. I had retrieved this earlier out of the Thomist view that a 'participated beatitude' inheres in all things by virtue of their origin in the Creator. But Berdyaev's view of the mutuality of the two freedoms is much more emphatic."*

Hand me the Vallon... (Handed the book, he searches it out and he reads). What I was trying to get at was there was an existential co-naturality between man and nature. His (Vallon's) view of the Thomist view was that man was stripped of divine grace and was only restored to it through the sacraments. Whereas according to him there was an existential correlation between man and nature which does not depend upon the sacramental redemption. It's the spiritual nature of man in extension, I mean, actuality and not a super extension of supernatural grace upon him. So therefore it (this view) permitted me to not have to depend upon the supernatural sense... But I know the same thing exists in Thomism. I think he oversimplifies a little bit the Catholic and Thomistic parts but he does it to emphasize something else. I don't object to it because it's what you have to do in discourse. In the Catholic and Thomistic conceptions you could easily find ways of accommodation to Berdyaev's perception, it's just a matter of where you want to throw the emphasis. That's why I say, at the beginning of that passage, that it doesn't make much difference because the Redemption is so great, so total, that it becomes an academic question in terms of what you want to do. But in terms of the poetry there's a difference because it has to do with the stance, the stance you take to the subject.

What difference would there be in the stance?

The difference between the Mother and the Bride.

In an article you wrote, published in The Catholic Voice, *you mentioned that...sacramentalism was a good basis for searching into totemism. How did sacramentalism help you enter into totemism?*

What I was probably trying to say there is that the idea of totemism isn't repugnant to me because the idea of sacramentalism led me to understand the nature of sacred symbols. I'm able to foot my way through the world of symbols. Because I'm able to retain my doctrinal adhesion to the Church and at the same time explore the animistic basis of the totem in primitive societies and to try to recover what they held fast to, what sustained them, but for me within the evolved state of the sacramental. There's a distinct state of evolution between the totem and the sacrament. In other words when Christ redeems humanity he redeems it through its needs and when he sees the whole of humanity straining towards totems then he emerges as a divine totem in his own right, which is in some ways more approximate to his own reality than ours. Whereas, before, the totem serves only a fundamental natural animism, the symbol operates at the same levels, in terms of psychology. You see what I'm saying? It's the same archetype whether it serves as totem or sacrament. The sacrament is just a more evolved form of the same archetype. That's why the totem doesn't scare me at all. It must have scared the pants off those editors back at *The Catholic Voice*. I called the article you referred to 'Poetry, the Totem and the Animistic Christ' but they didn't print that.

So it's something like the Corn King as the Christ...

Yes, it's the same thing only I take it back to a more primitive and American dimension. I take it from the European Corn King to the aboriginal American setting to get to the root forces working at life on this continent. That's what I was probing for. But I wasn't confused about whether I was serving some sort of animistic god or anything like that. You know, like the conventional idea of the sacrament as cannibalism. Well, all right. If people have a cannibalistic need then God knows how to reach them. God did it in the Redemption. What is that cannibalistic need that motivated so many of the tribal peoples? God knows what he's doing when he gives us his flesh to eat and his blood to drink. What I was trying to do was to translate that over to the American turf.

Since you're an American poet.

Yes.

Along these lines, regarding your interest in astrology, would this sacramental view relate to that interest?

Well, it might for some people, but not for me. I'd never really made that connection. No, there's a difference. There's a psychological difference. In terms of the totem your symbolism reaches down to the chthonic level, the infra-rational. See, you've got three planes of cognition (I'll be a Thomist now): the infra-rational, the rational and the supra-rational. The totem relates to the infra-rational but astrology relates to the supra-rational. It's a different level of symbolism. The mode is the same but the psychological plane is different. It's more conceptual, nearer philosophy than it is to religion. How do they relate? Well, the same formula applies to each. Like we said that the sacrament is the symbol which effects what it symbolizes, well, the same thing applies to the totem and to Saturn, the planetary configuration. They're both talking the same language but they're relating to different sides of the mind. One relates out to the cosmic order and the other relates back to the earth. There's much more emotion constellated in the totem and much more celebration and conceptualization in astrology. It's the difference between the gnostic and the aboriginal. Astrology is much nearer the symbolic range of gnosticism whereas the totem is way back down into the infrarational, going for the root, earthly energies. The planetary thing is closer to the angelic.

It sounds like what you were talking about in your interview with Albert Gelpi ('A Conversation With Brother Antoninus', The Naked Heart, 1992, University of New Mexico) about the difference between the shaman and the priest. The shaman going into the underbelly of society and the priest...

Yes, the shaman goes into the underbelly but I'm not prepared to say that the priest... The astrologer is closer to the magician in the sense that the astrologer is working with the occult forces, the outer, cosmic configurations and trying to bring them into a coherent, human pattern. The magician wants to do it for the sake of power. The astrologer wants to do it for wisdom. Of course you can corrupt astrology in the search for power and become a magician, you can use it in a magical way but that isn't it it's essence. Astrology is much more about understanding what's happening than about how to make things happen.

How would you reconcile astrology with your Christian faith? Do you see any sort of conflict there?

No. I wouldn't have been involved in astrology if I'd sensed any. I felt it was the same as the study of any other objective reality, like the weather or whatever. The fact that the sun rises in the morning is an astronomical fact, the fact that you get up when the sun rises is an astrological reference. Astrology relates what happens in the heavens with what happens on earth. Astronomy makes no reference to what happens on earth in relation to heavenly events.

What about the Tower of Babel and the prophetic warnings against the wisdom of the astrologers of Babylon?

Well, in the Old Testament, and even in the Early Fathers of the Church in the Roman Empire, there was a struggle against all forms of gnosticism. But in the thirteenth century under the influence of Albert the Great and with the rediscovery of Aristotle, astrology reemerged into Christianity under a different modus, much more naturalistically oriented. The competitive factor had been eliminated by many hundred years of the Dark Ages so the theologian didn't have the same pressure, the same speculative urgency, and so they could look at it with more detachment. Astrology was pretty much accepted by the church up until Copernicus, when all forms of utile symbolism went pretty much by the board with the collapse of the Ptolemaic system. Astrology was so closely identified with the Ptolemaic system that when the new system came in the older schema with its planetary baggage was simply dismissed. Thus the nascent science of astronomy became infatuated with the new telescopes and the new gadgetry. Even so it didn't happen over night. Leo XIII in the nineteenth-century was the last Pope to retain a resident astrologer, though more as a holdover from classical times than a practicing specialist. With Einstein there's a new perspective and astrology once again finds its own credibility. But it took the Einsteinian revolution to do it.

So in the Catholic Church there's room for astrology that doesn't seem to exist in the Protestant church.

I think that, if properly understood, astrology would be within that spectrum, also. The Protestant Revolt was just as much a revolt against the excessive symbolism of medieval Catholicism as anything else and it moved back toward the ethical dimension of the Gospel message. That's been the limiting factor in Protestantism, the repudiation of the symbolism. It's not so much that it's balanced it with the ethical, it's elevated the ethical out of all proportion to the symbolic. In some ways that's why it's boxed in today, because of the historic fear of symbol and ritual as being agencies of Rome.

So, getting back to astrology, how would you define it?

In the first place, it's not a science, it's an art — a study of the cycles of the planets, relating to cyclical time as opposed to linear time. Cyclical time is the recurrence of the eternal return: everything comes back together, recurrence based on the cycles. I mean you could throw chairs up into space and they'd come around regularly. You could make the same fundamental deductions from them. It's as simple as that. I mean there's nothing occult invested in the planet except in terms of the energy field.

There are titanic forces out there. Those planets are not just globs of dead matter. We know that. Take a basic concept of physics, the transmission of energy into mass. Something's happening, there's a transection of titanic forces. Where they intersect and intermesh there's a combustion, and a consolidation, and we call it a planet. That means it is the bearing off point of a whole field of active energies. They're the relation points of the moving forces of the whole cosmos. They're like floats on the Bay, you know, you see the floats go one way and you know the tide's coming in. The floats move another way and you know the tide's going out. Saturn comes around in its time and you know the tides are coming in. Jupiter comes around in its time and you know the tides are going out. You accommodate yourself to them just as you do to a weather vane. They're the same cyclical laws of existence that sustain the whole cosmos.

The other principle is the correlation between the unit and the whole, the microcosm and the macrocosm. The day I'm born I'm like a photographic negative and I begin with that imprint of the cosmic situation at the moment of my birth. My horoscope is a map of the cosmos at the time I was born which is a configuration of influences as emerged into consciousness, right? I bear these with me as my own personal signature. Everything in that chart has changed as the planets move but it's changed under tension. You can see the evolution of the psyche in terms of this abrasion of the cosmos upon the situation in which I was born and the cosmic evolution that goes on outside of it.

All these relate to the material and phenomenal world. Within this is the spirit of another dimension which is non- cosmic. That's the unique me, the unique person, which has nothing to do with astrology. Astrology only applies to the phenomenal world and the occult, or the as-yet-hidden, world. People try to grasp this hidden world and they revert to magic in attempting to integrate these forces back into life.The principle of spirit doesn't belong to the phenomenal world but it evolves in consciousness through the phenomenal world. The only wisdom I gain is through my sensory organism as it evolves in life, otherwise I go on from the same place I was when I was born, an inert consciousness in this plane of existence.

The only power the Satanic principle has over me through astrology is my ignorance of it. If I'm ignorant of it and bow down before it, and try to use it for domination that is the point in time at which the devil shows his hand. And it's easy for Him to do because that's his turf. His turf isn't in exoteric knowledge except through pride and vanity, but rather in the esoteric where you get your hot little hands on the controls of power. Then you can be sure you're getting close to the devil's realm. If you use astrology as you use the weather and knowledge of tides it just happens to work. That's how I use it.

Berdyaev is really opposed to the whole idea of fate. Do you see a conflict between his view and the science of astrology?

I would think of free will and choice as being the same as the other cosmic influences. The most powerful astrological ingredient is, of course, the moon, because it's the closest to us and has the most weight, therefore is the most easily verifiable influence. You can look around and see the difference between a society under a full moon and a society in the dark of the moon. I mean, the maternity wards fill up with the full moon in a way that they don't in the dark of the moon, as do the insane asylums. Within this tidal movement of natural contextual forces of the phenomenal world a person makes choices. There's always a limitation of freedom which is the context, state of life, maturity and conscious evolution in which we live. The child of five is going to respond differently to a situation than a person of twenty-one or a person of seventy-five, and so on. We don't think of these as violating free will but simply as conditions in which the free will operates. I'll say flat out as a Christian that no astrological influence is capable ultimately of overriding the free will of a person, if the will is truly activated and not somnolent. But there are so many esoteric influences on the psyche that the free will is overborne by emotional factors from within. And it's within these dimensions that the astrological influence is chiefly felt. These interior impulses and motivations seem to spring directly from our choice but are in fact part of the conditioned reflex. One of the great contributions Skinnerites made to Christianity was that they forced us to see issues we grandly assumed to be free choice are actually part of a conditioned reflex. They're forcing us to redefine our sovereign territory of where we are and where we aren't. They compel us to recognize how much of our free will is taken up into the contemplative rather than the active sphere. I don't use astrology to understand what's going to happen, although it would behoove me to do so, since it would save me much trouble in my life if I'd use it in an applicative way. But I'd rather put my trust in God. I look back twenty years and now I can relive the time when I was so passionately making money. To recognize and see my faults and not to live hounded forever by the furies of experience. Through consciousness and recognition to achieve accord and deliverance in the contemplative realm is free will. My capacity to relive my life in terms of my present knowledge is to me the supreme dimension of my free will. It's like, from the Buddhist point of view, the only way to be delivered from karma is through knowledge.

A CANTICLE TO THE CHRIST IN THE HOLY EUCHARIST

Written for the Feast of St. Therese of the Child Jesus, Virgin and Contemplative, 1953.

Gustate, et videte quoniam suavis est Dominus!
                                        – Psalm XXXIII

And the many days and the many nights that I lay as one barren,
As the barren doe lies on in the laurel under the slope of Mt. Tamalpais,
The fallow doe in the deep madrone, in the tall grove of the redwoods,
Curling her knees on the moist earth where the spring died out of the
        mountain.
Her udder is dry. Her dugs are dry as the fallen leaves of the laurel,
Where she keeps her bed in the laurel clump on the slope of Tamalpais.

Sudden as wind that breaks east out of dawn this morning you struck,
As wind that poured from the wound of dawn in the valley of my beginning.
Your look rang like the strident quail, like the buck that stamps in the
        thicket.
Your face was the flame. Your mouth was the rinse of wine. Your tongue,
        the torrent.

I fed on that terror as hunger is stanched on meat, the taste and the
        trembling.
In the pang of my dread you smiled and swept to my heart.
As the eagle eats so I ate, as the hawk takes flesh from his talon,
As the mountain lion clings and kills, I clung and was killed.

This kill was thy name. In the wound of my heart thy voice was the cling,
Like honey out of the broken rock thy name and the stroke of thy kiss.
The heart wound and the hovering kiss they looked to each other:
As the lovers gaze in their clasp, the grave embrace of love.

This name and the wound of my heart partook of each other.
They had no use but to feed, the grazing of love.
Thy name and the gaze of my heart they made one wound together.
This wound-made-one was their thought, the means of their knowledge.

There is nothing known like this wound, this knowledge of love.
In what love? In which wounds, such words? In what touch? In whose
        coming?
You gazed. Like the voice of the quail. Like the buck that stamps in the

thicket.
You gave. You found the gulf, the goal. On my tongue you were meek.

In my heart you were might. And thy word was the running of rain
That rinses October. And the sweetwater spring in the rock. And the brook
    in the crevice.
Thy word in my heart was the start of the buck that is sourced in the doe.
Thy word was the milk that will be in her dugs, the stir of new life in them.
You gazed. I stood barren for days, lay fallow for nights.
Thy look was the movement of life, the milk in the young breasts of
    mothers.

My mouth was the babe's. You had stamped like the buck in the manzanita.
My heart was dry as the dugs of the doe in the fall of the year on Tamalpais.
I sucked thy wound as the fawn sucks milk from the crowning breasts of its
    mother.
The flow of thy voice in my shrunken heart was the cling of wild honey,
The honey that bled from the broken comb in the cleft of Tamalpais.

The quick of thy kiss lives on in my heart with the strike, the wound you
    inflicted,
Like the print of the hind feet of the buck in the earth of Tamalpais.
You left thy look like a blaze on my heart, the sudden gash in the granite,
The blow that broke the honeycomb in the rock of Tamalpais.

And the blaze of the buck is left in the doe, his seal that none may have her.
She is bred. She takes his sign to the laurel clump, and will not be seen.
She will lie under laurel and never be seen. She will keep his secret.
She will guard in her womb his planted pang. She will prove her token.
She will hold the sign that set her trust, the seal of her communion.

I will feed thy kiss: as the doe seeks out the laurel clump and feeds her
    treasure.
I will nurse in my heart the wound you made, the gash of thy delivery.
I will bear that blaze in my struck soul, in my body bring it.
It keeps in me now as the sign in the doe, the new life in the mother.

For each in that wound is each, and quick is quick, and we gaze,
A look that lives unslaked in the wound that it inflicted.
My gaze and thine, thy gaze and mine, in these the troth is taken.
The double gaze and the double name in the sign of the quenchless wound,

The wound that throbs like wakening milk in the winter dugs of the doe,
Like honey out of the broken comb in the rock of Tamalpais.

Thou art gone. I will keep thy wound till you show. I will wait in the laurel.
I know as the knowledge is of the doe where she lies on Tamalpais.
In the deep madrone; in the oak; in the tall grove of the redwoods;
Where she lies in laurel and proves the wound on the slope of Mt.
    Tamalpais.

1953

Second Interview
Vocation, Witness, Encounter

This interview first appeared in *Radix Magazine*, May 1980.

•

Clifton Ross: *You've referred to the total effect of a poet in front of an audience as "the act of witness". In our correspondence about witness you once said that witness was in effect "a shift from linear to cyclic time". Could you explain what you mean by that?*

William Everson: Yes, but Berdyaev has made a point that blew the roof off my mind. He comes in and changes everything. I've been teaching "Birth of a Poet" for nine years now, on the tension between cyclical and linear time. Suddenly I read Berdyaev, who introduces the idea of existential time. To symbolize duration, he uses three figures: for cyclical time, the circle; for linear time, the line; for existential time, the point. For him that point of existential time is the eternal, the point that transcends both the cyclical and the linear. For me it is the point out of which witness emerges, and vocation, too. The power of vocation is the power of existential time rather than that of cyclical or linear. Heretofore the only way I could account for that power was to see it in the fusion point of the two. Actually that fusion point is existential time. I just didn't have the name for it.

So where the linear and cyclical touch, that is the point of witness, the existential point of contact?

Yes. It's also the point of personality, as Berdyaev says. It's the point of transcendence, transcending the linear and cyclical time or consciousness. It's the ultimate mystery, the X factor. You know it's there but you don't know what it is or how it is. There isn't any way to grasp it except by purely being it. You can become it but you can't know it. That's the great thing about the vocation: it takes you to the point. You can become the poet, you can write poetry, but you won't know why or how. You can draw on both cyclical and linear time but you can do that only by entering the point of existential time which is the point of coherence. And that's how art enters the subspecies *aeternitatis*.

You're saying the existential point is the point of vocation?

Let's put it this way. From the point of view of God, the existential, the eternal, the only way he's going to enter into continuity with the phenomenal world is along the line of his own modality. That is the existential time. Vocation is the line of his application of the eternal into the phenomenal situation, which is a convergence of cyclical and linear time. The principal way he's going to do that on a cumulative, continuous point of application is through the power of vocation. Vocation is an archetype, the mode of divinity. The continuous, non-miraculous infusion of divinity into the human dynamic is through the prophetic power of vocation.

"Archetype" sounds Jungian to me. I'm not familiar with Jung so I don't know

how you're using the word "vocation".

Vocation is a calling. I'm using it now in the religious sense. You're "called" to the ministry, you'd say in Protestantism, or you're "called" to the religious life in Roman Catholicism; every religion has its special calling. I apply that, in a secular milieu, to any occupation or activity that can be referred to as a calling. I say that denotes the charismatic factor in it. The charismatic, the transcendent, the thing beyond. You're called beyond your limitations. Society cannot evolve or progress on its own. It is inert. It can do so only through the charismatic calling, the vocation. In my view the whole of society evolves around certain basic vocations (such as that of the poet) which stabilize it and to which it always goes back.

You spoke of vocation as the way to divinity. Is that with a small "d" as one coming into one's own personhood?

Yes. But divinity with a large D is the term of your personhood. That's the greatest mystery of all. When the small d in you changes to the large D, you've got it made. Then they call you a saint!

Could you say a bit more about witness and "encounter"?

Witness is more of a permanent attitude but encounter is more of a situational stance. Encounter changes with the situation; witness is permanent. The witness stands behind. The same witness goes through encounter after encounter but it's witness that precipitates the encounter. They're two aspects of the same thing, but the witness is the perdurable attitude. The clash and response of that attitude in society is the encounter.

You've spoken of the poet-prophet's function as "effecting a displacement in the consciousness of the hearer". Is it the witness that effects that displacement?

Encounter effects the displacement, but witness supports and precipitates the encounter. Here's the world, wrapped up in its soporific pleasures and its karmic dream. The prophet is projected into that because he has entered the point of existential time. In cyclical time, nature fulfills its own law and has its own peace and acquiescence. Linear time has its gratifications and satisfactions. In the clash between them, the humanist says, "By conscious control I can manage both to my own ends". But the prophet says, "No! There's a third element, which is eternity". This is the encounter of witness, which interjects eternal time into the equation between cyclical and linear time.

As Berdyaev points out, linear time was invented with history. That aspect took me back a bit because from his point of view, history begins with the Incarnation. Up until then cyclical time was all-pervasive. I've always tended to think of linear time not so much as historical but as empirical, cause-and-effect time: I do this and that happens. I can't precipitate cyclical time; all I can do is accommodate to it. But I can precipitate linear time. Berdyaev says there was no true history until the Incarnation. He points to the Greeks as being disinterested in history because they were totally immersed in cyclical time, gaining all their knowledge and all their wisdom from their scrutiny of cyclical time. Personally, I would have thought that Rome was a vast extension forward into linear time, an attempt to apply power to the historical situation. Rome tried to create history through the application of the phenomenal world. I would see the Roman ethos as largely linear, but I don't know what Berdyaev would say about that. The crucial issue is the intrusion of existential time into the cyclical/linear tension.

Christ's Incarnation gave meaning to history. Otherwise there was only the cyclic; every attempt to change history was simply feeding back into cyclic time. But at the point of the Incarnation something unrepeatable and unique happened, so that linear time could be introduced from that fixed point.

Yes. The intrusion of existential time into the cyclical processes.

In one of your letters you were speaking of the Beat poets. You said they attempted the displacement but were unable to effect resolution. You went on to say that to this day that is a weakness of Allen Ginsberg. How does a poet, as you put it, "effect displacement" and keep it there?

First of all, I think of Christ's witness and how he refused to set up a kingdom in this world. You might say he took it underground and let the Holy Spirit be the operative factor through the conditions of the secular world.

I think the power of vocation is the stabilizing factor, though that may seem to contradict what I said about Ginsberg, whose vocation is certainly authentic. The obvious way to stabilize is through form. In fact the function of form is to secure the charismatic truths. Truths that have been arrived at through experience, through spiritual intuitions, are made durable only through some kind of formalization. Nobody likes an institution because it hems you in. But the only way humanity can retain its wisdom is through formalization; aesthetic, ritual, or social institutionalization.

The Ohlone Indians around here had no history because they refused to talk about the dead. But their world was so stable that they could go through generation after generation doing the same thing and having no need of history. They were a food-gathering people and nature was so stable in this area that they didn't have to rove, nor were they invaded over maybe ten thousand years. They just lived – until the whites came. Then their world was blown apart. But they didn't need history because their ritual was sufficient. What accommodated human time to cyclical time was that ritual. As long as you performed your rituals, which were maintained by taboo, you lived a complete life, and went on to the next world. Those are rudimentary institutional forms. Legalism is the evolution of taboo into proscription, but it's the same archetype – the attempt to achieve a structure against the ravages of time.

Of course, some people try to remain free spirits and let somebody else do the institutionalization. They try to retain the displacement by maintaining the primacy of the charismatic. They want to be lightning rods of the divine and not have to bother with the laborious process of institutionalizing. So they cut out, and in the aesthetic world they become bohemians. You know, Telegraph Avenue.

Well, you seem to "retain the displacement". How do you do it? I know that at the Berkeley reading people were still sitting in their chairs for half an hour after you finished reading.

Let me go back to Allen Ginsberg. By denying form Allen loses retention. He invokes the flash of insight but the powers of retention, which are the formal ones, he explicitly denies, refusing to rewrite. He pursues a new point of illumination rather than attempting to retain or structure illumination through revision. But eschewing revision means that he commits himself to very little retentive power. Insight is all he wants, and he's made a whole aesthetic out of it. So I doubt the permanence of much of his work. I think Allen is essentially a platform artist, that he carries his impact through persona and charisma on the platform. And poetry is more on the platform now than it is in the book.

Some of Allen's poems do have the formal power to retain the displacement. 'Howl' does and I think 'Kaddish' does too, but very few others do, especially in his later work. Those two are Hebraic, using Hebraic psalmic parallelisms, ancient literary devices, from an intuitive point of view. But Ginsberg doesn't do that much any more. Neglecting the formal powers, I think he lacks permanence.

As for myself, I move with the same appetite as Ginsberg toward the immediate, and the implications of the immediate illumination. Yet at the same time I use more formal devices in order to gain depth and retain it. One of my reservations about a Ginsberg appearance is that there's not much depth in it. He can elevate an audience to a happy feeling where they're all shouting "Right on", participating at that level. But for me the major communication comes through the silences. I think that comes out of my time in the monastery. In a sense my poetry is an ordering of silences. It does that through rhythms, through recurrences. All coherence, in a sense, is the formality of cyclic time because it's built on the principle of the eternal return.

That silence is an incredibly tense element, building to the poem. And also that casual discussion on the platform before you read: it's that existential moment coming back into the poems.

Something has puzzled me, though. I remember your saying that after your conversion a sudden burst of energy came. Yet most creative artists who become Christians seem to experience a lull in their work after conversion. How do you explain what happened to you?

I believe a period of cessation is normal after conversion, a sort of regrouping of energies. But for me, I was almost overwhelmed, as if there were a dam breaking, as if aspects of myself that had been pent up forever suddenly found their direction and were released. It was just affirmation, affirmation, affirmation, after all those painful years of being oppressed by the world.

Do you think that much of the tension people are trying to work out in their writing before conversion gets resolved with pat answers, so that they no longer feel a need to deal with those tensions?

No, it's more of an archetype. After any kind of momentous decision there's a natural cessation of energies, a period of banked fires. The classic conversion was St. Paul's, where you have that period of blindness and inarticulateness before he could swing into action. I don't know why I didn't experience that. I was suddenly taken up with the exploration of the new truths I had discovered. I immediately began to apply those insights to my familiar region. I'd take up Biblical incidents and establish parallels between Palestine and California, writing poems like 'The Making of the Cross' or 'The Flight in the Desert'. I'd use my California locale the way the Renaissance painters took Biblical scenes and set them in Tuscany. I'd been writing about the western landscape for years and suddenly, with my conversion, I brought a freshness to it. It was wonderful to experience.

Maybe there were some tensions that you'd never experienced before. Many of us have grown up in a church so we find it difficult to approach the mysteries in a fresh way. But you were approaching those tensions, and the ultimate tension, the Cross, for the first time.

Yes, that's true.

You seemed quite able to keep away from what some would call "propaganda verse". How were you able to do that?

Actually I got close to it in a poem like 'Gesthemani'. Then there's another one, a long poem that's never been published. *The Veritable Years* is dedicated to Mary Fabilli, who was instrumental in my conversion. It contains a sequence to her written at the point of our separation. Originally there was a long poem in which I became quite polemical. My editors advised me not to put it in *The Crooked Lines Of God* and when we were putting together *The Veritable Years* the same advice was reiterated. I agree that it lost its poetry by being dogmatic.

Was that 'Springing of the Blade'?

No, the sequence is 'The Falling of the Grain' but that particular poem was 'The Summer of the Flesh'. You see, by the time I entered the Church I had my poetic equipment well in hand. I'd published a lot of poetry and my versification was honed. So it wasn't that I was struggling with the problem of craft. I knew how to say exactly what I wanted to say and I think the poetry was saved from the convert's zeal mostly by its emphasis on nature. I drew on natural imagery, the energies of nature, and also, to some degree, on the erotic. I simply seized on the elements the usual Christian convert is suspicious of. A new Christian's poetry often tends to be abstract, idealistic, and ethically oriented. Those are hard things to get into poetry. Poetry needs concreteness, sharpness. But by sourcing it in the passions and in the landscape I fought shy of that. I also drew on the power of affirmation, which is suspect to "modernist" poets.

For instance, I wrote 'The Wise' as a direct refutation of T.S. Eliot's poem, 'The Journey of the Magi'. I was taken aback by its modernist skepticism. The magi had come all that way, but looking back on it they ask what did they come for? Was it a truth or was it a fiction? It was because I was so scandalized by that doubt that I wrote my poem with such ringing affirmation. I had the magi goading their camels at breakneck speed. And they

> flung themselves down in the dung
>   and the dirt of that place,
> And kissed that ground, and the tears
> Ran on the face where the rain had.

That breakneck precipitation was the way I was feeling. I think that ingredient made my poetry different from the usual conversion poetry.

That ingredient was affirmation?

The breakneck affirmation of those poems.

You mentioned "Modernism". I take it you're speaking not so much of modernist theology as the modernist poetic movement. You've mentioned once before that much of the difficulty one has in writing religious verse is rooted in that movement. Were you referring to its skepticism?

Yes. Modernism is essentially skeptical. It's cool, detached, ironic, stressing form over content, suspicious of affirmation. But I followed Robinson Jeffers and D. H. Lawrence, two masters who never succumbed to the modernist dialectic. So when I finally came to a body of belief I could affirm I didn't have the problem of skepticism to inhibit me.

Some people speak of "a Christian poetic". What do you think of that? In your own poetry, did you notice any major shift after your conversion? You've mentioned the periods of silence when you read on the platform, coming out of your monastery experience as a new addition to your reading. Were there accompanying changes in your writings?

No. Only a shift in content. That one feature, the silence, was a platform thing. The last poem in *The Hazards Of Holiness*, 'In Savage Wastes', began to incorporate those silences into the writing. That poem was built around a series of koans, you might say. Each stanza tended to be a self-contained unit, so in reading it you could put as much time between them as you wanted to. In the elegy to Jeffers, 'The Poet is Dead', I actually made that an operative principle. I went so far as to put asterisks between stanzas in order to accent those silences. That was the major change in my platform experience instituted as a poetic device. Other than that I can't recall any stylistic changes.

So you don't believe there's such a thing as a Christian poetic?

No, I do not. Somebody might persuade me if they could show it to me. But I'm not aware of it. In fact, I resist the idea. I hope there isn't.

Berdyaev would be in agreement with you. He says that no laws govern creativity. But he also says that Christian art is romantic art, always trying to break through to the transcendent.

Where did he say that?

In The Meaning Of The Creative Act. *But then again, T.S. Eliot's poetic voice changed after his conversion. In 'The Wasteland' that voice was desultory and fragmented. After his conversion the voice became more definite, more immediate, less fragmented.*

But the thing there is that he shifted over to classicism from modernism. It wasn't so much a Christian poetic as a classical one.

What do you mean by "classical"?

Well, formal, in the sense of less oblique, less fragmentary, more direct, more formally whole, more formally resolved. Less suspenseful, more thematically developed. More intellectual, with less emphasis on the sensibilities.

Most people are unfamiliar with poetic criticism. Many who don't know what is meant by Modernist poetry just know that they don't understand it and don't like it. Did Modernism start with Eliot and Ezra Pound?

Before that. Both of them drew from the French Symbolists. That influence was coming from the intellectual situation in Europe at the turn of the century, chiefly the situation in science where advances had placed the humanist ideal on the defensive. The triumph of post-Newtonian science was so total that people thought little place was left for the human spirit. Religion was deemed a fiction. There was no God and anti-transcendentalism was rampant. The anti-transcendental, anti-romantic, anti-humanist emphasis of modernist poetry replaced the transcendent with irony, with a bleak, cold view of the human situation. It put down human aspirations. It moved against the romantic cult of personality and the sublime and tried to register the diversity of fragmentation through the splintering of form. That's one reason people stopped reading modern poetry. It was incoherent, fragmentary, arcane, detached, superior. That alienated the general reader who had been oriented around Romanticist poetic reservations. Modernism attacked those norms and did so on the basis of the prestigious science of the time.

Then of course, along came Einstein, whose relativity in science threw the whole cosmic bag back toward the transcendental. Yet the prestige of Modernism was so great, and still is, that it's taken all this time to get a neo-Romanticist movement going. Dylan Thomas was the first neo-Romantic poet following the Einsteinian revolution.

Why would you class Dylan Thomas as a romantic?

Because his work is passionate rather than ironic; celebrative rather than deprecating; libido-oriented rather than intellect-oriented, transcendent rather than concretized. He adopted a few elements associated with Modernism, like surrealist techniques, but rather than using them ironically, he used them in a celebratory way. He stole fire from the enemy. Most people probably find his work obscure, too, in its limited paraphrasable content. But Modernism had reduced the paraphrasable content to nil. It is Romanticism that has striven to make poetry as articulate as possible. That was why I held against Modernism all the way through, because I had the intuition that it didn't square with reality. Not with reality as I experienced it.

You said in one interview that you'd be willing to sacrifice the perfection of a poem in order to make personal contact, to encounter the audience. That statement would sound like heresy to a Modernist, I gather.

Yes, for a Modernist poet, it would be poetic heresy.

I'm still exploring the idea of a Christian poetic. Just from the fact that the Modernist sees the world as fragmented and chaotic, and writes that way, I'd say that Modernism wouldn't square with a Christian specification, to fit the content of the Gospel that has meaning, continuity and order, into such a fragmented form...

Well, there might be exceptions to that, but I can't think of any. In other words, if you start to define a Christian poetic it would include the idea of an adequation of form and content. It would have to be transcendent. It would witness to a reality superior to this phenomenal world. But then, Romanticism would say the same thing.

Since the Incarnation is central to Christianity, in some ways Christian poetry must be incarnational. By that one means the divine "bodied forth" in the human, in the material. But I don't think there has to be a perfection of form for it to be Christian. In many of my poems I move toward a rupture of form as the liberation of the charismatic, the numinous. In many poems I've celebrated the emerging of Christ out of the anguish and agony of the ruptured forms. That's one of the witnesses of the crucifixion: the divine is sought not only in perfection but also in imperfection. And the crucifixion witnesses to the essentiality of violence.

As in your poem, 'In All These Acts'?
Yes. One reason I'm not a critic is that I place emphasis on the violent, attempting almost to canonize violence as an operative principle. I point to Christ's saying that "Heaven is taken by violence, and the violent will carry it away" as part of my own "Christian poetic".

When I reviewed The Veritable Years *I mentioned Incarnation and encounter as aspects of your poetic. Do you keep in mind, as you write a poem, the personal encounter with the audience? Is that a major aim in your writing?*
In the sense of the blaze of mutuality that encounter exacts, it is. And it is not only a movement from the poet to the one encountered. It's also as Berdyaev said: God needs his creatures to encounter with, to reveal an aspect of himself he couldn't realize in any other way. That's as much the reason for the Creation as any other. Encounter is necessary for complete self-realization, self-awareness. So prophets consistently seek for their own clarification. The Good Shepherd seeks his lost sheep as much for his own need as for the needs of his sheep. That's true of the artist, too. Artists seek the subject matter as an encounter with themselves.

I've been speaking of this aesthetic in terms one is used to regarding as masculine: encounter, thrust, displacement — all being aggressive. Yet when I wrote 'The Encounter' I spoke in terms we think of as feminine: receptivity. That's one reason why it's so difficult to talk of a Christian aesthetic. Almost every form can be accommodated to Christianity because of its universality.

You just mentioned prophets again. I've read an interview between you and Albert Gelpi in Sequoia *in which you spoke of poets as prophets. That was confusing to me. In the Old Testament there were true or false prophets, as in our own time. They weren't deemed true or false by any standard of poetic merit but by truth or untruth. It seems that often a poor poet could be a true prophet, whereas a good poet may be utterly false as a prophet. Isn't there a kind of danger in equating poet and prophet?*
Encounter is the central role of poets in their culture, as I stated in the *Sequoia* interview. They are to effect displacement in the normative consciousness, in order to institute a new advance in the evolution of the culture's awareness. At the same time, poets are healers. They wound in order to heal. They jar with encounter and revive with resolution. I'm not sure I can focus on your point about the danger of considering poets as prophets. Whether a poet is good or bad is a qualitative question but whether a prophet is true or false is a moral one.

Well, I know you've regarded poets as prophets in the sense of shamans who descend to the "underbelly, going down into the unconscious, where the tribe is troubled". What do you think of Jacques Maritain's book, Creative Intuition In Art And Poetry?

I can't quarrel with the reasoning in it. Both Maritain and Thomas Merton think of poetry as a rung on the ladder of contemplation in the ascent to the Absolute. They see the poet as a contemplative making an ascent to the divine, and see art as one of the modes of that ascent. My problem with that view is that it tends to make art more and more refined as it gets to higher and higher phases of being, and I don't think art works that way. The whole idea of ascent from the gross to the refined is a very formal and classical way of looking at things and tends to emphasize form, reason, and the ideal. Whereas they see artists as contemplatives, I see them in a prophetic role. I see artists as conduits of the divine overflow back into the contingent. That accounts for the whole shift in perspective of what the aesthetic is and does. Through rupture and violence, the divine intrudes into the contingent. A lightning flash from the heavens to the earth is much more the way I see art. It accents the elements of strain, rupture, violence, anguish and pain. Out of that comes the idea of encounter and the artist as prophet confronting an audience, the hearer. Art finds its verification along that mode: from the absolute down, not from the contingent up.

I guess you're talking about the poet as archetype of the prophet, not prophet in the strictly Biblical sense. And you've laid out two wholly different approaches: the Thomistic ascension and Berdyaev's passionate, suffering God is a theme that you and Robinson Jeffers have both dealt with in your poetry. Is that theme very much a part of Romanticism?

Yes, it is. Jeffers built his whole aesthetic around the idea of the stress or creative tension between the divinity in nature and nature itself. The revelation of the strain in nature was, for Jeffers, the clue to the secret of it in art. He went with an unerring instinct each time to that point of rupture and violence as the breakthrough to the noumen, the divinity inherent in the physical object. It was through Jeffers that I saw God in the cosmos I and became a pantheist. It was through Mary Fabilli that I began to break with that Jeffersian pantheism when I began to see God in Christ.

A CANTICLE TO THE WATERBIRDS

Clack your beaks you cormorants and kittiwakes,
North on those rock-croppings finger-jutted into the rough Pacific surge;
You migratory terns and pipers who leave but the temporal clawback
    written on sandbars there of your presence;
Grebes and pelicans; you comber-picking scoters and you shorelong gulls;
All you keepers of the coastline north of here to the Mendocino beaches;
All you beyond upon the cliff-face thwarting the surf at Hecate Head;
Hovering the under-surge where the cold Columbia grapples at the bar;
North yet to the Sound, whose islands float like a sown flurry of chips upon
    the sea:
Break wide your harsh and salt-encrusted beaks unmade for song
And say a praise up to the Lord.

And you freshwater egrets east in the flooded marshland skirting the sea-
    level rivers, white one-legged watchers of shallows;
Broad-headed kingfishers minnow-hunting from willow stems on
    meandering valley sloughs;
You too, you herons, blue and supple-throated, stately, taking the air
    majestical in the sunflooded San Joaquin,
Grading down on your belted wings from the upper lights of sunset,
Mating over the willow clumps or where the flatwater rice fields shimmer;
You killdeer, high night-criers, far in the moon-suffusion sky;
Bitterns, sand-waders, all shore-walkers, all roost-keepers,
Populates of the 'dobe cliffs of the Sacramento:
Open your water-dartling beaks,
And make a praise up to the Lord.

For you hold the heart of His mighty fastnesses,
And shape the life of His indeterminate realms.
You are everywhere on the lonesome shores of His wide creation.
You keep seclusion where no man may go, giving Him praise,
Nor may a woman come to lift like your cleaving flight her clear contralto
    song
To honor the spindrift gifts of His soft abundance.
You sanctify His hermitage rocks where no holy priest may kneel to adore,
    nor holy nun assist;
And where His true communion-keepers are not enabled to enter.

And well may you say His praises, birds, for your ways

Are verved with the secret skills of His inclinations,
And your habits plaited and rare with the subdued elaboration of His
intricate craft;
Your days intent with the direct astuteness needful for His outworking,
And your nights alive with the dense repose of His infinite sleep.
You are His secretive charges and you serve His secretive ends,
In His clouded, mist-conditioned stations, in His murk,
Obscure in your matted nestlings, immured in His limitless ranges.
He makes you penetrate through dark interstitial joinings of His thicketed
kingdoms,
And keep your concourse in the deeps of His shadowed world.

Your ways are wild but earnest, your manners grave,
Your customs carefully schooled to the note of His serious mien.
You hold the prime condition of His clean creating,
And the swift compliance with which you serve His minor means
Speaks of the constancy with which you hold Him.
For what is your high flight forever going home to your first beginnings,
But such a testament to your devotion?
You hold His outstretched world beneath your wings, and mount upon His
storms,
And keep your sheer wind-lidded sight upon the vast perspectives of His
mazy latitudes.

But mostly it is your way you bear existence wholly within the context of
His utter will and are untroubled.
Day upon day you do not reckon, nor scrutinize tomorrow, nor multiply the
nightfalls with a rash concern,
But rather assume each instant as warrant sufficient of His final seal.
Wholly in Providence you spring, and when you die you look on death in
clarity unflinched,
Go down, a clutch of feather ragged upon the brush ,
Or drop on water where you briefly lived, found food,
And now yourselves made food for His deep current-keeping fish, and then
are gone:
Is left but the pinion-feather spinning a bit on the uproil
Where lately the dorsal cut clear air.

You leave a silence. And this for you suffices, who are not of the
ceremonials of man,
And hence are not made sad to now forgo them.

Yours is of another order of being, and wholly it compels.
But may you, birds, utterly seized in Gods supremacy,
Austerely living under His austere eye—
Yet may you teach a man a necessary thing to know,
Which has to do of the strict conformity that creaturehood entails,
And constitutes the prime commitment all things share.
For God has given you the imponderable grace to be His verification,
Outside the mulled incertitude of our forensic choices,
That you, our lessers in the rich hegemony of Being,
May serve as testament to what a creature is,
And what creation owes.

Curlews, stilts and scissortails, beachcomber gulls,
Wave-haunters, shore-keepers, rockhead-holders, all cape-top vigilantes,
Now give God praise.
Send up the strict articulation of your throats,
And say His name.

1950

Third Interview
The Poet and The Prophet

An interview of William Everson meeting with the Artist's Group of the Tenderloin Reflection and Education Center, July 6, 1983. This group included Jim and Carmen Neafsey, Joseph De Rugeris, John Collins, Robert Lenz, Rey Culaba, myself and others. I have attempted to identify the interviewers where I was able. However, this turned out to be a nearly impossible task since the transcriptions took place over ten years after the interview. I regret omissions due to the passage of time and in advance make my apologies to those whose names I've left out. This interview first appeared in *Poetry Flash*, August, 1994. The tape begins with the interview in progress. The interview took place under the High Embrace at Kingfisher Flat, just outside of Davenport, California.

•

William Everson: ...I don't think anyone's ever tried to do that before, identifying the seven virtues with the persona and the seven deadly sins with the shadow. But when you think about it the persona is the projection of our own ideology, the best we want or can make of ourselves so it just about has to be that way. Depth psychology has been so secular that it doesn't know how to use that religious heritage. I won't belabor the point, but I think I have a first there, psychologically. Then I'll justify the need for understanding how the negative and the positive profiles match up and interlock. And it's a lifelong interlocking because neither one will go away. They're both permanent fixtures in the psyche and they turn out to be the bearing off point. You see, polarity is the principle of consciousness. No polarity, no consciousness. That's a Jungian fundamental. So you always look for the opposite. In fact, oftentimes you can tell more about a thing from its opposite than from the thing itself. Because there's a blinding factor in the ideality about what we hope for ourselves or try to establish for ourselves. You touch a virtue and it bites. It has to be that way because it relates to the basis of polarity. You might even go so far as to say that the vibration between these two entities is what consciousness is.

Jim Neafsey: *In the interview that Albert Gelpi did with you on 'The Poet as Prophet' you talked about your need to surrender to your own vulnerability as part of the call of being an artist. That seems to connect with the shadow thing. Or in* The Birth of a Poet *you talk about the power of the negative. Just what does that have to do with the quality of poetry, the acceptance or the surrender to one's vulnerability and negativity?*

I think the question is answered in that polarity problem. The whole idea of surrender is the problem of the persona, the idealization which goes one way. And you can't tell what your vocation is until you somehow tap into the other side of your personality. It usually comes at the end of your adolescence. Schematically, we think by the age of twenty-one, when a person can vote, that they'll have everything fairly well in line. But it just doesn't happen that way.

In religious terms, unless you lose your life you can't gain it. That conception of Christ's. It's the losing of your life which is the principle of your Selfhood.

The ego's formed against this framework of ideality which we get from the culture. The persona is highly stressed because of all the shames and evils and hurts that are our lot in life – not to mention the respective traumas we've all repressed. And the psychic energies have focussed around the shadow, the negative profile, and it gathers weight there. The longer you live the more weight it carries until you turn around and face it. And it's this turning and engaging which is what is meant by "jumping through your shadow". It's to let go of your conscious discipline and embrace the dark brother inside of you, the dark one, the Cain.

Clifton Ross: *I'd like to pursue the idea of the poet as prophet. The prophet of God is right, and infallibly right, so he can actually say 'Thus saith the Lord'. Now a poet can be a great poet but, like Pound, he can be wrong. Pound's analysis was wrong.*

There's plenty of historical evidence of false prophets. You mean the poet as a failed prophet or a false prophet?

Well, I'm just wondering if there's not a distinction between the poet and the prophet. The prophet could of course be a great poet but...

Not necessarily. Sometimes he doesn't even speak. He works it out with his toe in the dust. Poetry is a gift of expression and it can augment almost any of the subjects it can amplify. Of all the arts it's the one peculiar to language. They say that music is the greatest art because it's the most concentrated aesthetically. But literature specifies in a way that music can't, and it's this power of specification, in language itself, which is it's greatness. It can almost always rise above it's own limitations, above its own rhetoric, if you want to put it that way.

Prophesy is essentially about being visited, which you can't induce. The problem of ancient Israel was that it placed its dependence on the prophets. It was sort of like the aboriginal peoples wherein the whole tribe depends on the presence of the shaman because he has the link to the powers. So in the evolution of religion you get the situation of Israel in the Old Testament where the prophet voices the charismatic, takes the role of the shaman in the sense that he's the link, the connecting point. And this is why the false prophet was so hated and excoriated; because everything depended on the truth.

I think the prophetic angle in poetry is the insight that comes through the visionary experience. It's the visionary moment, when the poem begins to emerge out of your banked memorial deposit and the other obscure shadow areas that lie in our unconscious. Back there where the correlations have been intensifying. This is a kind of prophesy because the problem is always the sacred and the profane. The sacred which is pure and simple and the profane which is complex. This process of correlation, which goes on in the unconscious, is the area from which both the poet and the prophet work. It's just that the poet here is a kind of prophet of the aesthetic. The medicine man and the desert prophet are not so concerned about that aesthetic. But the fact that such good poetry has come from such prophets, like Isaiah, who is ranked as the greatest religious poet the world has seen. The Catholics say Dante, but for my money it's Isaiah because there's the naked encounter.

The shaman knows encounter, too, but it's the encounter with the demons, the devil. The prophet is the encounter with God, with the positive rather than the negative because it's the social role that he occupies. And this social role occurs at a level forward of the presentation. The prophet, per se, is not thinking of himself. He's thinking of the plight of his people. And it's in this public concern that these unconscious correlations begin to synthesize and it becomes a burning issue in him, so that he has to speak, because he's burning, burning with the pain of his people. This, per se, is not quite what the poet is. The poet is speaking personally. It's coming from him where he's saying, "this is the way it is with me. Make of it what you will but I'm speaking".

Isn't that where you'd see the social function of poetry? That out of that one person's experience something is universalized? That they would represent a whole society?

What you say is undeniable. But there's some difference in degree between the selflessness of the prophet and the selfliness of the poet. They come out of the same place but the accent is different.

Just for clarification, (Jerome) Rothenberg, if I'm not mistaken, would put the prophet and the shaman in the same category. You mention the prophet as conversing with God and the shaman as conversing with demons. Would you want to separate the two then?

The shaman has his own formula. The aboriginal peoples worked out their solutions to problems in similar ways. The way one tribe, for instance, resolved a problem, was the same as another tribe. So there was a commonness of technique between them. And the technique of the shaman was to follow the person who was sick and the whole community would get in on the act as support. And the shaman's job was to go down to the nether world, meet the soul of this afflicted person, which is headed for the Great Beyond, and to then rescue it and bring it back. The shaman is much more like an analyst, a therapist, in that sense, only it's a collective event. But the penetration and the utilization of the unconscious in a charismatic way is the function that ties the poet, the prophet and the shaman all together. That's why, in *The Birth Of A Poet*, I say "Shamanize! Shamanize! Get with it! Stop fooling around, pushing one word here and another word there! Jump through your shadow! Shamanize!" And I use that because the counter culture is more interested in Native American approaches than they are in the familiar biblical heritage. Therefore, in our society, the poet is closer to the prophet.

Neafsey: *How about yourself, Bill, in your own work? In that same article on the poet as prophet you were talking about moving more towards the shaman in your post-monastic phase. How do you see your own vocation?*

Well, I'm nowhere near the prophet archetype as I was in the Order. It has to do with your aspirations rather than your achievement. On the other hand, my bid for the shaman, the fascination with the primitive, is a sign of decadence in a society. But yet you have to live with your own context and if we're decadent enough to be re-exploring the primitive, then we'd better do it well and make it count. That's what I try to do.

The way I got into it was through the problem of the prodigious persona. I had become so identified with my monastic image when I read the effect on the audience was massive. Even as the poet on platform carried a compelling force. Some people say that in the quest for sanctity you're supposed to eliminate the persona as an artificial construct... Well, let's put it this way, when I took off the habit and got up on the reading platform I found myself feeling utterly naked, as if I had no identity. I didn't know what I was going to do. I didn't feel like dressing as everyone else because I didn't feel it as my own. My role as a poet had called me to a charismatic vocation which I knew as distinct and for which I'd found an ideal persona, as a religious poet, which is the monastic habit. And the power of it was that the collective had put it on me. I assume for myself, as I had to with the shamanic persona, that the power of the monastic habit is authenticated by the collective with full confidence and support. I thought that what I was going to do was to clothe my unconscious self, make my persona out of my own antediluvian valuation and try to use it in my quest for understanding life on this continent, how it should be lived. So I began to go back to the North American Indian who'd worked out the intensive life-style of physical survival on this magnificent continent that we've turned our back on and are now coming to a crisis point with our environment because we have turned our back on it.

There is a strong long-standing tradition which holds that the persona is antithetical to spiritual life. This tradition focuses on the reflexive action of the persona as the individual encounters values on his quest through life.

A while back I read the biography of Tolstoy. In the latter part of his life he adopted the garb of the peasants. When you read his life it's apparent that he was no more a peasant than I am a mountain man. He turned all the business of running his estate over to his wife. What he said was 'I wanted to walk away from it all but the family said no'. So he turns it all over to her and she runs it just like a noblewoman in the aristocracy would. And he sits there day after day in his peasant outfit and the religious pilgrims come and talk to him.

I never have felt like a fraud with my buckskins, just like I never felt like a fraud with my religious habit. If I'd adopted this when I was a younger man I might well have felt that way. But after those long years of persona identification in terms of career... It's true that the American poet is prone to eccentricity because he has no real standing in the community, although you might have a high academic standing if you're accepted as a teacher. Auden says that in England the poet always thinks of himself as a clerk in the establishment, and he identifies with the rulers of the nation whereas in America every poet thinks of himself as an aristocracy of one. And so I'm your local shaman. I earned my buckskins, as much as any Britisher has earned his Laureateship.

Neafsey: *Were you saying that as a younger man these values that you have, might not have been so authentic but now they seem to fit, or the buckskin seems to fit as something that symbolizes part of your life?*

Yes, as something I've touched, drawn, as something that's available to me, not just for my ego...

Neafsey: *What is that? Could you say more about what those values are and what that buckskin symbolizes?*

When I was a young man I was going to be a poet and a farmer. I was going to make my living, identifying with the California earth. The archetype there would be agricultural, not so much the "good peasant", in the Tolstoyan sense; but we'll say, as the British would say, the good "yeoman", a vocation founded on tradition and the relation to the earth. You see this nowadays as American like in Wendell Berry's approach, given his relation between his poetics and the environment.

But when I left the Order I couldn't go back to that. I had to step down to where Thoreau was, at one with the wilderness. Thoreau says, "in wildness is the salvation of the earth". My origins lie in Jeffers and that's pretty much where he was with his whole elevation of the cosmos, untouched by human hands, as being superior to us with our profane misconception. Jeffers had a very strong persona and he dramatized it to focus his energies on the redemption of the earth.

Arriving here in the Santa Cruz mountains was a perfect solution to my quest. I had gone first to Stinson Beach and then got the call from U.C. Santa Cruz and came here. I got some good poetry out of it but the poetry isn't going in that same line. I began that line in the first book I wrote at Stinson Beach, *Man-Fate*, and there is a more naked quest. There's not really any search in *The*

Masks Of Drought from here on. It's more or less reflections on the relations between psyche and nature, unusual events or untoward events in nature. There's a psychic correspondence developed into it, what Gelpi called in his review, 'The Landscape of the Psyche'. Which is where I got that negative profile from, 'The Landscape of the Psyche'.

Neafsey: *One image that comes to mind. I was reading some Jungian work, I believe it was Maria Von Franz, talking about Merlin as a figure who withdrew so far from society – to the edges of the wilderness, to touch this deep, psychoid level, the level before nature and psyche get split, something beneath the cultural symbols. I was feeling something like that for* The Masks Of Drought, *like in* The Veritable Years *you use a lot of Christian imagery, cultural imagery and those kinds of derivative symbols, but then you get to something simpler and deeper and almost pre-symbolic, like seeing the mystery in the physical facts.*

That's a very great compliment. If it's true, yours truly is great because it doesn't happen very often. There's a kind of 'daimonic' – when you were describing that area I got almost a pulse, a twinge of the preternatural vibration, that vibration which is the obsession of the charismatic person and the one that the mystic listens to. I don't get that from the poetry. At least not from *The Masks Of Drought* but I'm glad it's there. This has something to do with the preoccupation with violence and the agency of violence in the charismatic calling. Somehow, when you go down to those obsessions, the recourse to violence comes to hand and if you can't subsume it into an aesthetic form, or formalize it into some dimension of purposive social action, the dangerous maniac arises. That might be a very good description of where he's coming from. He's close enough to the obsessions to be touched by them in the sense that the insane are called "touched". Hence it goes without saying that the charismatic poet is likewise dismissed as one touched.

Ross: *That's what you meant by the shaman and the devils as opposed to the prophet and God?*

Yes.

What does the prophet do instead of accosting the devils with the shaman?

He rebukes them too. But he has a spiritual heritage and the collective support to channel it in a positive way. If he doesn't have that he could very easily be mad. Because you don't go into those realms unless you have an awful lot of protection. That's one reason I was so grateful for that period in the Order when I finally had to go into the unconscious. I had almost a perfect laboratory in which to do it. There was the support of the community, the competent spiritual counseling, there was the ever present religious atmosphere to keep you in balance. But it took seven years of that kind of support for me to reach the place where I could do it. I know I could never do that again. And if I hadn't done it there I don't know that I could have done it anywhere, at least not to the same degree. That's what's the problem with the thrill-seekers. They go into the forbidden realm without preparation for a vision. For the drugs are effective. They do take you there. Which is their great danger and risk.

When you enter the unconscious that way there's always bound to be a great deal of inflation that comes surging forth, an incredible inflation that comes when you go through one of those breakthroughs and you see things you've never seen before. Then you become, for a while, what Jung calls a "mana personality", and a deep commitment is made for the rest of your days. You run preaching, born again. In his latter days Thomas Merton was deeply disturbed by *The Seven Storey Mountain.*

So is it really possible to synthesize the institutional and the charismatic? I guess the institutional and the charismatic is another way of saying form and content and the genius pulls this off but always goes beyond what the institution will allow. Is it really possible to unite those two?

But that's always been the cross. The relation between the charismatic and the institutional is defined by the cross. This is the cross that Jesus said you have to take up and carry.

De Rugeris: *I wanted to know about Christ as the symbol of the Self.* The Masks Of Drought *seems less explicitly Christian in its imagery, but perhaps more Christian in its incarnational reality. I guess I'm more asking about your own experience of Christ since you've left the monastery, how that's shifted or developed. It seems like there was a dramatic experience of Christ in your conversion, and yet, where has that gone?*

Well, there's less ego identification with it. But that daimonic element, the preternatural, that's where Christ is.

Neafsey: *That deep psychoid nature/psyche level?*

That's where the energy is, both the spiritual and physical energy. There are almost no symbols for it, but almost being presymbolic. You use terms almost like electric, terms of higher sensation.

Joseph De Rugeris: *That's where the primal is? So it's more of a cosmic sense?*

No, not cosmic, for me cosmic is vast, large scale. That's why I was never much interested in cosmic consciousness: it seemed vaporous, madly inflated. But this other thing, penetrating and informing, I'd once identified it as sex under the Freudian aegis but I no longer do that. I once identified it as love, but I no longer do that. There's a danger there, like when you have to work with highly dangerous material in chemistry. But I don't feel the need to pursue it as a quest the way the chemists do. Although it could well be that that's what the quest for the Holy Grail was all about.

I think that figure of Merlin that you brought out is interesting. It's the same thing in *The Masks Of Drought* when I was thinking I was going toward the aboriginal I ran across all these medieval, Camelot figures. In some way there's got to be the negative factor there to make it tell. There's the theory that consciousness is a disease, and finding an analogy of a polarity and the vibration between the opposites is like a filament, then consciousness is a pain and a prolonged pain is a disease.

Ross: *[Lev] Shestov says that, too, that rational thought is a result of the fall, the ability to think in terms of good and evil. If I didn't know you better I'd call you a Maoist because that's what he's talking about. Motion and growth and evolution are a result not of external factors but of internal contradiction and, quoting Engels, motion itself is a contradiction. In the west we think of everything as externally motivated, but in fact it's more a complex of internal contradictions.*

Question: *Is contradiction really the same as polarity?*

Depends on your definition. The mind thinks of them as contradictions. Contradiction has more of a negative factor. What would you think is a better word? In your view are they more at peace with each other?

Same person, responding: *Not necessarily more at peace with each other but one does not negate the other. Paradox as opposed to contradiction...*

I see what you mean, conceptually.

Ross: *I think Mao means it more in the sense of paradox. More as polarity.*

De Rugeris: *Sometimes in your work, you say, you are aware that it is flowing out of a different space, let's say a space that is more in harmony with yourself.*

Probably the contradiction is something we have to get over to see the harmony.

Neafsey: *Even with something like* The Masks of Drought, *as you were saying, often the poems were inspired by some point of tension or violence or some unusual happening but frequently they seem to break into some experience of harmony or mystery at the end of it. It's almost like the contradiction opens out into something where there's a reconciliation or transcendence or something.*

That's the Self, the emergence of the Self.

Neafsey: *So those are the touch points where the primal reality breaks through in some ordinary event. That why, when I was asking about the cosmic thing, as you spoke, I thought, no, it's something much more intimate than that, something in a small, ordinary occurrence that issues out into something large. But it's something small and ordinary rather than something vast and airy. I wanted to get back to that. When you talked about primal reality you said you once identified it with sex but you no longer did that. Nor do you define it as love. How would you define it?*

I love love. I live in love. I think that just about makes the difference of it because love is personal in the highest sense of the word. Whatever this other thing is, is more daimonic than I associate with Christ, but it's become the vehicle for my instinctive reflection about Christ at this phase of my life. Maybe just because it's more creative.

It's nothing that I think of in terms of my own creativity. There's a certain inspiration that you go through when you're creative that takes the place of love and domestic life. You can create all day as long as you're not tired; as long as you're not bored you can keep on loving. But this other thing has to do more with whatever that psychoid state is. Meister Eckhardt had this idea of a primal Godhead that lies beyond the Trinity and Jung associates this with the psychoid in the psychological equation. It's the *terra incognita* in Jungian studies. He [Jung] got into it very late and it was only Ira Progoff that wrote a little bit about it.

This daimonic business, which makes it almost by definition, the preternatural, which I'm not too interested in identifying that way. It covers too much of the non-causational types of activity with poltergeists. I tend to identify the preternatural with the occult. What I'm trying to specify here I hadn't thought too much about until you asked me where, at this point of my life, do I find the Christ. What that thing is, what that is that I find to be the principle. Actually, in terms of the Trinity, the psychoid couldn't be the second person. Godhead couldn't be the second person. But those distinctions all blend away, given the nature of our minds. In that sense of the unity of all things I began with as a pantheist. I'm getting back close to it in the psychoid. That word primal we were tossing around earlier, Eckhardt's *urgrund*, the ground, not so much as the earth but as basic.

De Rugeris: *Bill, you've looked at your own life as thesis, antithesis and synthesis. Would you go into that? It might get us closer to this primal reality. What was thesis?*

Thesis was Nature. Antithesis was God. And the synthesis was God in Nature. In *The Masks Of Drought* Nature is primary and God is indicated but behind the scenes, you might say. There's a retention of liturgical nomenclature throughout, words with only a religious association, like "cincture" or the "sacrificial host" between the river and the woods in 'Spikehorn'.

I've pretty much mined that vein out now and I'm moving along a different track. I got into this big epic in which I was supposed to look over my life, but I tend to distrust the fact that it's too programmatic. I think that that's why I've been dragging my feet in relation to it.

In art they always keep pointing to things like Beethoven's last quartets as being the supreme attestation of the synthesis phase. Or Shakespeare's sonnets. Those rarefied but at the same time thoroughly substantive works like the

Quartets that might not even be his best works. The Third Symphony is hard to beat of its kind. That was a young man's storming whereas in the last symphony you'd have to be deaf to compose it. If he hadn't been deaf, if he hadn't had that affliction we couldn't have followed that view of what reality is. Parkinson's [disease] is getting me there fast! Faster than I want to go, actually. It's happening on platform more than it is in my writing. The incredulity, when I finished the reading there at St. Boniface and I got that round of applause that almost blew me back... I said with all genuineness, "You've got to be kidding." That's closer to what that transpersonal thing is than when I write. I daresay that's the way it's going to be. I'm not too interested in rarefied states of being. To me it's the direct contact, almost the physical encounter. I'm a man of sensuality whose affirmation is – you saw that article in *California Living* that had the headline across the top that said "California's Prophet of the Physical". I would have said, "California's Mystic of the Flesh".

De Rugeris: *Could you tell us a little bit about your technique, Bill, how an image gets transposed or transformed into a word and a word into a sentence?*

It's mostly a matter of rhythm. You find the rhythm and the rhythm begin to find the accommodating word. There's a pulse or vibration within you that says "it's time to write". You get up in the morning to write and you're moved yet you have no ideas. Then the rhythm begins to establish itself and the words adapt themselves out of the storehouse of your memory, tending your delight in what that rhythm is doing. And it's out of this that the image corresponding to that rhythm begins to take shape. And the image is just the beginning, because we haven't got to the concept part of it yet.

Oftentimes, in beginning a poem, I'd write a few lines that didn't make very much sense. I'd cut them out later and begin the poem in a more direct way. But after I went through that "Dark Night of the Soul" phase at St. Albert's, and began to work on *The Hazards Of Holiness*, I began to leave those lines in there because they seemed to have an unconscious correspondence that was fitting, if not necessary. Something like 'Gags Thrids'. Bring on one poem that way, then under that another line and another... "When the Devil can't find a way, He sends a woman. So does God."

De Rugeris: *So what you're saying is that it's an unconsciousness that moves you. It's not a decision to write.*

Yes, it's like defecation. You know when it's time to go. But you know you're onto something when you go back to it. That's why, although I identified with the Beat generation, I didn't go for their automatic writing. To get the true flesh of that unconscious tilt, Kerouac would try not to change the words at all. I was opposed to that tactic because I practice another way. The Beats didn't accept me as one of them because my poems were too closely worked over.

Ross: *Same way with punks now – their focus on "raw" music.*
Question: *Is there a fear of reworking, that reworking would mean structuring, which would mean bridling, which would mean a loss of spontaneity?*
I think those are all operative there, yes. But my own notions of creativity, especially on the basis of that movement, that the first draft is not able to keep that cohesion to the rhythm in play throughout, but by reentering it and receiving it afresh you pick up on those lapses and fill them. That's why I don't consider it an overlay, because of its capacity to take you back to itself. So its second vibration is as good as its first, if you know what I mean. That's my view of creativity. I think [the Beats] are too much informed by drugs and the highs you get from those. I think the drug phase put a blight on creativity, on true composition, because that peak experience was thought of as the ultimate and so the language had to do the same thing whereas from my point of view that's a mistake. There's only one great poem that I know of, 'Kubla Khan' by Coleridge, written under opium, but even with that poem, which is a *tour de force* of its kind, you're glad that all literature doesn't confine itself to that proclivity.

Ross: *Isn't there something valid there, though? Just in terms of breaking through the societal conceptions of the world, the normal framework, normal state of mind. Alan Watts, in one of his essays, talks about how while he was taking LSD everything became suddenly relevant. Now that's a problem since not everything can be relevant or everything becomes irrelevant.*
Yes, Alan Watts. His hope for LSD was that you could substitute the preparation for vision by varying the dose. That way you might telescope a long preparation for vision into a few hours or a day's experimentation. I imagine there's something about his Zen experience that might make him think something like that… But what's essential is the preparatory work: the prayer, the meditation, the sojourn, the loneliness, especially the loneliness; the quiet, the silences.

Neafsey: *There's something else I wanted to pick up on. It came out of that conversation about the salmon in the fish pool knowing their habitat, about it being imprinted. I know in your own poetry you talk about regionalism and region being imprinted and how you become the voice of that region. Could you speak about that and about some of the special problems with that today? Is it more difficult to be a regional voice today?*
I think it was more difficult under Modernism but now with the counterculture and the environmental movement I think it's going to be the coming thing. I think we're going to come back to a regionalism with a much higher consciousness than what it was before when it was just kind of "scenery". I don't want to fault our ancestors because I think a John Muir truly saw God in nature. I think he really was a prophet.

But I want to talk more about the problem of creativity and my feelings about the drug culture which was responsible for new standards in terms of what aesthetic content is. It's partly speculative and ideological because of Olson's projective verse which governed the writing of that period. I identified with the Beat because of its Dionysiac character. D.H. Lawrence, who was one of the culture heros of the alternative society, especially during the sixties, I think would not have bought Olson's projective verse theory. He was an apostle of open form, too, and he had specifically denied craftsmanship. It's a strange thing because, as a Virgoan, which is the sign of the craftsman, you'd think that Lawrence would be a super craftsman in his work. He disclaimed that and threw himself bodily on the intuition. He was essentially a novelist and only secondarily a poet and that's one reason he could do that, because he was sustained by his major work as a novelist and he could let his poems be tentative arpeggios of intuitive elaboration.

Jeffers did that too with his narratives. He'd write the narrative and there'd be little spin offs from it. He thought of these as supporting the narrative, almost a cluster effect. He'd like his book to be narrative and poems together in one volume because all the explication it was going to need was in those poems.

That's not Lawrence. You can't get that feeling about his poems, the correlation between the poems and his novels. Lawrence was a marvelously intuitive craftsman. He has an ear for his unconscious. Virgo not only rules the digestive tract but also the solar plexus. And it kind of figures that Lawrence was the prophet for the solar plexus for his phase in history. He tried to live by the solar plexus which he identified with the Pan force in nature and reality as opposed to Dionysus, which was much more physically based than the Dionysus with his wine, his mental conditions which Lawrence wanted to get away from, the mental conditions that distract or distort the movement of the physical. His idea was to get back to the solar plexus, which is a wonderful idea.

I take myself to be that kind of a Virgoan who rescues from perfection... Perfection from perfectionism. Perfectionism begins to become involved with its own absorption in detail being this kind of a worked surface. You can always tell it: Perfectionism is sterile whereas perfection is radiant. When you reach that point of radiance it's better that you stop with that than to try to bring everything up to a given level of finish. Actually, you really can't when you're at that stage of revision. You have to keep all the drafts. To me nothing is worse than to get rid of the drafts. Some people get rid of the drafts because they don't want to go back, to be distracted by the drafts. I could never do that. If I can't go over those drafts and see a better way of doing it that I missed when I first did it, then I'd feel I missed an opportunity.

I'm not afraid of the mind overlaying the mystical, the way so many who want to live spontaneously and prefer to live that way are so afraid of habituation as opposed to spontaneity. I've never been afraid of that. It's seemed to me always that the build for perfection is going to have to take both things. Just because it's better, if you see that first draft, the setting down the essence of the thing and getting the blush of it that you want, then you know its truth and its power for you and its relevance and the experience it came out of is illuminated but not completed...

•

I'd like to talk a little about the two challenges, complementary forces in the psychology of the artist: one I call the thrust for vision and the other is the thrust for recognition. I want to talk about the way these two forces complement each other, and the way they interfere with each other sometimes and what the danger points are there. It's easy to want to simplify and some very great poets have denied the thrust for recognition entirely. Emily Dickinson disdained it. She said "Publication is not the office of the poet. The office of the poet is to write." I think she was seriously mistaken. It's almost like that 'one-two' business we saw in terms of the opposites. Once we chime in on the stroke of vision and the poem begins then the stroke on recognition immediately picks up and resonates from that chime. And the reason for that is because of the consequentiality of the original conception. My view of the poet as prophet is that (this is a Jungian principle) society can't advance of itself; it can only advance through the charismatic person. But the rigors of this mean that it takes a heroic consciousness to sustain the inertia of the people you're talking for and the abrasive and negative force of resistance that makes you something of a pariah immediately comes into play.

If you refuse pariahhood, as Dickinson or Hopkins did – I think they'd both be bigger poets if they'd have published their poems and submitted to the verdict of their time as to what those poems were, even if they had to endure the same rejection that Whitman did. Whitman, who was a contemporary of them both, was the only one of them to take the thrust for recognition full faced. He did everything possible to get his work recognized, even before it was written. In fact he's a scholar's field day because when you gauge his life against what he created and what he thought of himself and proclaimed himself, touted himself and advanced himself, shamelessly, utterly shamelessly...

When I was in the Order and having to cope with the problem of trying to succeed on platform at the same time retaining my humility, the way they kind of put it to me there was that if you're doing something that's obviously a promotional work there's nothing wrong with that. If you start palming off a critical work of your work as if it were from some authority other than yourself, well, that isn't so good.

When I first began to go on platform after I entered the Order, about seven or eight years after the San Francisco Renaissance came, the platform had emerged as a primary vehicle for publication. This was mostly because we were so far from New York that our work just wasn't being featured back there. So we went on the platform and took the poetry field away from the academics by taking it out of the cloister and putting it in the hall. This meant publicity and it meant something of the cult of personality. At first I resisted that because I was afraid of it. But it was the Kennedy sweep that won the election in 1960 that made me change my mind because there was a case of a Catholic getting elected when there'd never been a Catholic president before him. And the Protestant hostility to him was immense. But the time was ripe and he understood it and knew it. It wasn't ripe when Al Smith tried it in 1930 but it was ripe this time and he knew it. And then he went to work and they got their whole organization up and with a matchless pace and expertise it was a hand-crafted political sweep. It was his greatest accomplishment because it was the most signal thing that he did. The rest of the things – he might have made some innovations on civil rights, but a lot of people did more than he did there – but no one did what he did, of equalizing the religious. Because America truly couldn't realize its final democratic ethos as long as those restrictions prevailed.

That made me see that if I was going to go on the platform I'd better go for broke because that was the only way you could do it. So I began to do my own publicity. I even went so far as to print my own posters and ship these on ahead of me. I highly touted myself. I used all my photographs and I shamelessly used all the good blurbs that I had, I repeated them over and over. I'm a skilled typographer so I pulled it off with taste, which Whitman wasn't able to do. He was a printer but a hell of a one. By employing these three factors: my literary, my platform and my typographical skills I built up the image of Brother Antoninus. Then that problem with the persona which we got into earlier became a factor.

Now this thrust for recognition as a concomitant of the thrust for spiritual vision. It's the ugliest, and at the same time, most inflating and heady. If you become overprotective about it something is nullified; if you become excessive, like Whitman, then it militates against your witness after you're gone when people discover just what kind of a showman you really were behind the scenes. That's why I tried never to let that... that's one reason why I'm willing to let this other book [*The Rages Of Excess* by David A. Carpenter (1987 Wyndam Hall Press)], with its negative profile be published because it has to do with my perspective on the truth and ultimately, my fearlessness for those natural things to have any final say over you. Because the Freudian interpretations on Whitman I read were to me so profound and finely applied that I realized that it only added to his stature rather than detracted from it because they could trace his excessive need for recognition back to his early problem in the family with a weak father and a powerful mother who was in love with the first son and he wasn't that first son.

In fact, I bear a lot of guilt and I don't think it's going to go away because you violate certain things on that persona, especially in a monk and a religious, when humility and facelessness is what you're supposed to present to the world... But on platform that won't work if you're going to draw. If I go out for a reading I want to draw as heavily as I possibly can. I'll use almost anything to draw a crowd because I know I'm not superficial on platform and therefore the more people I can get in there the more people I'm going to touch, that can be moved by what I have to say. I'm the same way with printing, when I print a book for Lime Kiln Press I feature myself as a master printer, which I am, but you're not supposed to call yourself that.

Part of the psychological point there, and maybe it's just rationalization, but what I used to say is that I can proclaim anything for myself as long as I can live up to it. To me that's the sign of the emptiness, that you can't live up to your own billing. And sometimes you don't. Sometimes you fail your billing.

Here in the Bay Area, at the beginning of the San Francisco Renaissance, *Time Magazine* in 1959 had a feature on me called "The Beat Friar". The local Archbishop urged my Order to silence me. He demanded they silence me all over the country but they stood by me. He wouldn't allow me to read in his diocese and this meant that I wasn't showing around San Francisco at the time the greatest focus of attention was on it. So I was reading all over the country except at my home base. That meant that my home country hadn't been exposed to my personal techniques, my platform style. I'd go into the Midwest where they're personality starved so to speak anyhow. They'll acclaim you as much for a personality and you know damn well what you're being brought in there for is personality reasons, and you have to use those things to get your message across. Because, if you waver and begin to simply celebrate yourself and don't get on with the business of changing hearts and changing lives and changing attitudes then the bid for recognition has won out over the bid for vision and you fall into the easy success. The devil tempted Christ with this very same proposition. I also developed an encounter ingredient in my readings that didn't get exposed in San Francisco. In other words, I'd do anything to encounter the audience, to break up that negative pall that people get when sitting expectantly when awaiting an event. You know, that wooden look, the terrible blankness, they're just content to sit there surrounded by their kind, just the terrible, absorbing eyes. For me, the minute I'd get out there I'd start to stare and I'd walk back and forth on the stage and just look the audience over. By this time some of them would be getting the willies and they don't know whether to run or stay or is he drunk or what's happening? That worked in the Midwest, not so well on the East Coast where they'd tend to resent a little bit this presumption.

John Collins: *You very effectively did that at the University of San Francisco. You gave me the willies.*

That's the point of the story. By my not being able to read around San Francisco the other poets had never been exposed to my act. And when I finally appeared on the San Francisco scene, there was a grass roots poetry reading. The press never picked up on it. But I began to get a lot of flack from the other poets. One of them was Allen Ginsberg at Grace Cathedral, this was late, about 1967, and I'd been able to read around San Francisco for quite a while. The archbishop had died a couple of years after he silenced me. (I always said the most dangerous thing an archbishop can do is suppress a poet!)

So at that reading with Allen he opted to read first. I didn't want to have to follow Allen Ginsberg. Ordinarily I'd prefer to finish on a big reading because it gives you the power of the closure: you can sum it all up and leave it all with an emphatic impression that they won't forget. They might forget others who read but if you have the closure and you do it properly they're not going to forget you. So I didn't know what I was going to do, following Ginsberg.

It didn't turn out like a normal reading. It was '67, the Flower Children year, everything was open, free and informal. Informality was the thing of the day. And I work from a more formal structure. I like to make an encounter group where everybody is brace-backed and then start to move in on the audience. And there's that negative factor which is always going to be there that you have to bring it out and neutralize. And this negative factor is seen in terms of the resistance to you: the more pressure I'd put on the audience the more you could see the resistance growing. Then you have to time it to a certain point, the break-over point and you know if you go beyond this one you're going to lose it all. And at that point I'd break down to a more accessible dimension and from here on out it's just peaches and cream. The thing I got from the platform, which is that contact with the audience, that love, actually, that is a form of love, the release of that love... It just takes a charismatic person to get it there because the collective doesn't have the power to do it itself, it has to be led to it. This experience of the totality of the love, which is always the keynote in the close, but to get to that point I had to do some fighting. I had to challenge the audience and get them out of this bland expectancy which they have. Actually, the audience invests a great deal of emotion in an unconscious way in the situation: you're the teacher and they're the learners and you're the one they've come to see. And no matter what anyone in the audience tries to do to you their sympathy is almost always with you. You've got the primary position and the audience is going to give you that.

Well, with Allen, what happened was, all his cohorts were out there and it was a very Beat/Hippy crowd, singing along, clapping and hollering with him.

He'd play a musical instrument, chant another poem, another mantra. When I got up there there was no movement, in other words, the expectancy of that still, flat conformity had been utterly dispelled by Allen's charismatic way with the audience. What I tried to do was play a trick from Noh Theater. You make an exaggerated, stylized gesture to let the audience know that this was going to be a different act. First I gave them a long silence. They'd never experienced anything like that though they thought they knew everything. I then went into something I'd never done before or since: a series of stylized acts, the function of which was to show the difference between what Allen did and what I was going to do. It fell flat because it was exaggerated and stagey and over formalized. Susanna, my wife-to-be, was there, and she said I flopped. The way she put it was "that was just bad".

I finally got through that and then went into my own reading. When I couldn't get them to be still, my silence wasn't communicating. They were breaking it up with catcalling and meowing and I turned on them and said "Who do you think you are? They know more in Kansas than you do." I kept punishing them until they began to hush. And when they got silent I went into my other part, what I had come to do.

To me I left the platform feeling vindicated because I got out of them what I wanted them to give me, too, but also because the nature of the response to me seemed indicative of anything but a bomb. But that did me more harm among the intelligentsia in San Francisco than almost anything I've ever done before or since. Essentially the same aesthetic strategy that had worked all over the country hadn't worked there. They were utterly unprepared for it.

(Bill takes a break for something to drink)

My feeling is the thrust for recognition ought not to be pursued too strongly until the age of thirty-five because the history of American letters is full of the people who have cracked up, who have got too much fame too fast before they attained maturity. The excoriate exposure to the collective mind that the prophet has to go through takes all his wisdom, all his experience and all his genius to maintain his sanity.

If I hadn't gone through that psychic break in 1956 when I had that breakthrough into the unconscious I wouldn't, first of all, have had the message, and second, I wouldn't have had the ego-strength.

Neafsey: *Could you talk more about that breakthrough? That was the time you met Victor White, wasn't it? What happened?*

White was already gone by the time I had the breakthrough. The first year that he was there I was over at Kentfield where I was a clerical novice training for the priesthood and I didn't meet him. When he came back the second year I worked out at the seminary at Saint Albert's and I got to know him. We had an instant sympathetic relationship and he became my mentor. We'll have to distinguish between the mentor and the ideal. You need an ideal to follow as an artist and this is the important thing, to get that prophetic figure to lead you into the unconscious. It's like Virgil leading Dante into the Inferno, that protective spirit. He's the ideal, but the mentor would be more like the coach. Whereas Jeffers was my master, [Kenneth] Rexroth, who hated Jeffers, was my mentor and I had this kind of opposition to work through. One of the things that doomed the Renaissance of the late 'forties was this problem. The people who are deeply in your life, like your lovers, feel threatened by the presence of the mentor, because he sees where you can go in terms of the strategy of the day, what's dying, what's old hat, what's new and coming and how you should bind yourself to it. Your lover resists that because it's a new and disruptive thing in your life. She doesn't want any changes of a radical nature. So hostility develops between the anima, the muse and the mentor, the politician...

White became something of the mentor for me at that time. He'd written a book called *God And The Unconscious*, which the Jungians have just re-released with my introduction and if you want to know about my relation with White you can read about it there. But I wasn't buying the depth psychology approach in those days. Under the great zeal of my conversion I was suspicious of Jung and suspicious of Freud. I was under very great pressure from spiritual aridity, the savor had gone out of my vocation. I was going through a very obvious period of the dark night of the soul, the night of aridity of the spiritual life when all the savor dries up and you're just going along by sheer effort. White thought I should go to depth psychology for the solution to this problem and I resisted. But then he left, and, since he was a light traveller, he couldn't take all the books he'd got for review so he gave them to me. And one of them was a synopsis of the Freudian point of view, laid bare, direct and concise: *Eros And Civilization* by Marcuse. I began to read that synopsis and at the same time I got a request from a professor who was putting together an anthology and wanted one of my poems called 'The Raid'. He asked if I could write a note or so explaining what my intentions were in the poem. So I started to write back and say that it was a poem written about the precept that those who live by the sword will die by the sword. It's a kind of Pearl Harbor scene. The planes come in and the pilots see the island down below them as a kind of feminine image in the water. They peel off and do the rape act, then there's the upstart inflation and they turn back to the ocean and the fleet is not there. The carriers have abandoned them. Then I said, wait a minute, because I'd just been reading Marcuse on Freud, and suddenly my eyes began to start out of my head. I began to see the Oedipal situation behind the poem which I had never suspected.

And it was this which led me into a dream of my mother and the next morning when I got up I grabbed a pen and started to write. I didn't attend any offices for the day, I just stayed at my desk and wrote. It was the emergence of the anima as the mother, only she was not a serene, nourishing mother but rather the eros factor that flows between the mother and the first son, because the first son activates that anima principle in her and she projects all her displaced erotic energy and he becomes the receptor. And this he bears into adolescence and it alienates him from the father and then his problems with women and father figures become greatly impacted. And then things like this poem get written. But when I pulled back the veil the anima emerged in her full sexual dimension, this was after about six years of celibacy. The uprush of libido is fantastic and what I did was write it out and act it out like you would a piece of pornography, just swept up in a sexual daze, a re-swearing back into sexuality after I'd forcibly put it out of my psyche for all of those early monastic years. I hadn't been tempted sexually in those years, that was really no problem at all, but once I'd opened the unconscious all that changed. From that point on I had to deal with the sexual factor, in my relations with women and with superiors.

Well, I wrote it all out that day. I got up the next morning and by a kind of instinct started the same thing all over again. And I did that for three days, wrote the same thing over, experienced it three times. Each day a progressively more chthonic version of the anima, and on the last day she went directly to the animal nature, emerging as a puma, a cougar, and I killed her at that point.

I went down to Mass the next morning. It was a Saturday. In those days we didn't have a community Mass. Each priest had to say a mass on the private side altars and each one had to have a server. One of the main functions of the brothers was to serve Masses every morning, assigned to a particular priest. I went down to serve his mass and he took the paten and put it on the chalice and laid the Host on it and he took the little Host and laid it there beside it and I just broke up. For the first time the gush of emotion began to pour out of me and I was crying. And he turned around to me and asked, "Brother Antoninus, what's the matter?" and I flung myself in his arms and said, "I've found the Father, I've found my Father."

At that point I was in the unconscious. There was no longer any point about whether I should or shouldn't: I was engulfed in it. Day after day, sorting it out, it just went on until finally I had to face the problem of my own anima, the animus, the homosexual factor that has to be faced out sooner or later and accepted and which came through at that time. I was going a mile a minute without any real help because Father White wasn't there to see me through it, but I was writing him letters. Some Freudians say you can't do a self analysis because there's no transference. In analysis you project the figure on the analyst and this is called transference. It allows you to flesh out the repressions in the unconscious because he is your anchor. Without this you can't get the job thoroughly done. It's just going to be kind of half-baked.

But I know that's not true because Freud didn't have a...

Carmen Neafsey: *Yes, who did his, right?*

Yes. Not only that, but when you have God, there's your anchor. I was reading Freudian books very assiduously but then I read Erich Neumann's book *The Origins Of Consciousness* and that was the book that threw me back into the camp of the Jungians and I never left it since.

It's like night and day, the differences in your life when you go through something like that. It's like a conversion in the sense that you have that 'born again' feeling. It has its inflations and its dangers and you do things that you'll later regret, but you'll understand. And this is more important, that you'll understand than that you'll live perfectly. That was preliminary to my public emergence. In fact, it was the thing that enabled me to start going out of the monastery more and more. Those first five or six years I just hung in there and kept the world out and I felt threatened by every new invasion of the monastic discipline. For instance later that first summer at Saint Alberts they got in a t.v.. and I blew up and walked out on them. Thought they'd ruined the whole Dominican Order. I returned after a few days and they accepted me back. But I was going through those sorts of things.

Ross: *What was that thing you wrote for three days? Was it a poem?*

No. No, more the way of a diary. It's in the Bancroft [Library]. Apparently what I'd done was I'd written it all out and then I'd made a typescript of it. I haven't seen it. I have no desire to go back and read it again. Those who've seen it have said it's so nasty, and yet so compelling... I was getting an awful lot of enchantment.

And that's one of the reasons I feel that depth psychology is not really a speculative thing for me. It was something I had experienced. I hadn't been able to see that poem [The Raid] for what it was. My attempt to get at the negative profile was, well, you can see what was happening there. I'd written that poem apparently objectively but to the trained eye everything in it had a symbolic nature of a condition that was being masked or hidden, repressed. Which is what you have to do in order to grow up, right? There isn't any other way to grow up without the victimizing or blessing of our condition.

Joseph De Rugeris: *I find it very curious that, after the three days of letting the anima emerge, the first thing that happens is finding the Father. When you said you "killed" it, you didn't mean that you'd killed the anima, did you?*

She has to be killed. There has to be a symbolic death there.

Carmen & Joseph: *The anima?*

The anima in her extremity.

Neafsey: *So that she doesn't possess you. Something has to break the tie there.*

Yes. It's like slaying the dragon. The funny thing about that is that, we've all heard about, following Freud, how you want to sleep with your mother. And you look at your mother and say "No way! Not mom!" (*Laughter*). But when she comes from the unconscious that way she's different. She's radiant and the erotic vitality and the sensuality are incredible. It's no holds barred. Then with this constant reduction down to lower, more chthonic elements she gets to the place where psychologists say she has to be slain to be delivered from. That's why they pick on the mysogynism in my poems.

Neafsey: *Does a similar thing have to happen with the father, that kind of slaying?*

It never took that form. I never had those sorts of problems with my father but with my mother. I was the first son and I got the cream whereas with my father I was suddenly a rival. In many ways I stole his bride. He broke with me when I became a conscientious objector in World War Two and towards the end of those three years he passed away. And I permitted him to die unreconciled with me. He'd sent a token toward the end...

What happened was that in the later years he was a judge in a small town where I grew up. He had to run for office and one of those campaigns for office came during the War when I was in the C.O. camp and this problem came up about me and he went around denouncing me. He didn't really formally disown me in the sense that he didn't cut me out of his will, but the reality was I refused to take his money and I was just as culpable as he was. The thing about the autobiographical epic is trying to get down into all that. He's changed from a negative to a positive figure in my mind now. It's partly from having to raise a child and in some ways the only way you're going to get through the Oedipal complex is when you have a kid of your own. Then you get it on the receiving end.

Our psyches have been structured by civilization in the long history of the race to work those things out. Because you can't make a civilization out of them, that's for sure. And yet when they're assumed and accepted they're the great balancing forces that civilization needs to survive. If it doesn't order the flow of its unconscious along almost ritualistic lines it's going to become very thin and superficial.

WHO IS SHE THAT LOOKETH FORTH
AS THE MORNING

Rising among the stampings of the sea.
She shakes the lifting light about her throat;
Her arms keep coolness with the stinging breeze,
And waves cup to her like a heeling boat.

Floating a risk of tresses on her nape
She wades the drift, and shaken of it, sways,
Treads riftages of brine, and treading swings;
She clicks her fingers on the birth of days.

Her shoulders sleek of sunlight and her breasts
Sculpt sea-troughs from the shoals of running seas;
Her narrow ankles split the stunning surf,
Barracuda slashes landward through her knees.

Lips glitter prophecies in waterlight,
Chromatic glints, bright oceanic flame,
Presaging triumphs and the doom of kings;
They sigh submission when she breathes their name.

Visage to visage, brow to burning brow,
They will fall forward through volcanic fire,
Rapt in the shudder of her vast embrace,
The drench of her insatiate desire.

She is the Mother of Life, Mistress of Death,
Before her feet the tiger coughs and dies,
And the bony elephant gives up the boast
Of those vast passions that once filmed his eyes.

Savage and awesome as the birth of suns
She treads a tumult on the stippling shore,
Churning the fleets of caliphs through her thighs,
And drowning the sailors that her daughters bore.

She is the Mother of Life, of Death the pride,
Nothing in nature broke that Maidenhead:
Man's glory entered life between her knees,

Yet does she keep inviolable the Bed.

Svelte goddesses usurped her place, but fell
Sweating with lovers in a flint embrace.
She holds herself immaculate apart;
The Spirit's expectation burns her face.

Yet lovers all must wanton of her will;
Out of her passion children shoulder birth.
The savage grips her in his groaning wife;
She takes her tribute of the teeming earth.

Dung and all darks are hers to ordinate,
The thirst of mules, the semen of the stag,
Beat of the flesh and the flesh's diffidence,
The sperm-swift cusp'd in the dreaming bride.

When lances break the ridges of the bone
Hers is the hand, and when the widow weeps,
Hers the invincible will that took the man,
Shovelling the tall dead for her windrow heaps.

She is the Mother of Life, the Queen of Death,
Her only Lover lives beyond the skies,
Coming to cover under the lightning flash,
The impregnation of the prophet's cry.

Upon a night of geysers by a sea
When the dead lay listening in their soundless pall,
And angels, fallen, shrilled the monody,
Strophe on strophe of their ancient gall,

She was accosted on a lonely hill
By what no man conjectured: in her womb
She bore the impact and the sacred Seed:
Pure passion broke the spectre of the Tomb.

Fire and thunder, fury at the source,
The blood's distemper and the mystic cry:
She took the wild Lover face to face;
She drank the danger of the brutal sky.

Prey of the lightning flash she dropped, consumed,
A votive-victim and a sacred feast;
Spun to the black and leopard-throated wind,
The spirit cupped her like a roaring beast.

That was the night the Son of God was struck
Deep in man's flesh, and left the body stunned;
Thrown by the Holy Spirit's aching lust,
Godhead and woman incommensurately oned.

What she gave birth to was halved of herself
And halved of Spirit, and would offer proof,
Searching God's cross out through the stark event
That immolates her instinct in His truth.

And when He mounts the cross-hilt of her flesh,
And nerve to membrane, joint to muscle bleeds,
She spits the seeds of passion through her teeth,
And sucks the wound that in His body seethes.

All night the little foxes cry her name,
In dunes beyond the sentinels of the streets,
But the gaunt Cross, divested of its love,
Milks blood like stinging rain between her teats.

Hewn of the digger's art, the stony slot
Seals flesh her womb kept like a doubled fist,
The man wrapped in His bridal cloth prescinds
The indentured breed from Time's slab-guttered list.

Now in the night the lovers seize her shape,
Each in the other's arms compassion taking.
Storming God's gate they hurl their lives aloft,
And harrow hell with that tremendous slaking.

Bride and the bridegroom, stroke on stroke surpassing,
The sexual agony or the heart's contrition,
Evoke the awe, induce, draw down the dream,
Compel the Spirit's awesome dereliction.

She is the Mother: in her womb the God

Burgeons Himself anew and tramples death;
And lifts her, plunging in the blaze of birth,
And shutters with His lips her surging breath.

Fourth Interview
The Engendering Flood

Thirteen years after the first interviews David Fetcho and I are returning to meet with Bill Everson. David Fetcho is one of the central figures in the poetry movement which evolved around Everson's work and through his inspiration. We discuss Everson's themes which are manifested by paradoxes he calls the "X factor", the mystery. The conflict, for instance, between the Apollonian and the Dionysian tendencies in art, between the intellectual, classical, institutional, academic tendency (Apollonian) and the erotic, romantic, bohemian and charismatic tendency (Dionysian), a conflict which has characterized Everson's entire life and which underlies all he other conflicts and contradictions. Inescapable? Everson would shrug and simply say, "it's the Cross".

There are, for instance, the contradictions in Everson around sex and violence, themes which would have to be treated separately. In terms of sex, Everson spent the better part of his life celebrating Eros in his poetry, much of that verse written while he was a celibate monk in the Dominican Order. As regards violence, Everson, who spent a number of years in a work camp for conscientious objectors during World War II, once stated that "...it is apparent that any strong preoccupation with apotheosis means that violence is bound to emerge as a positive, if unconscious, value". (*Archetype West*, p.13, Oyez Press, 1976). The contradictions multiply but they are those of a powerful person, one who understands the complex, contradictory nature of Truth and attempts to live it out.

We arrive at Kingfisher Flat late morning. It is raining. We come in just as Bill is preparing to eat the breakfast Steve Sibley, his friend and live-in aide, has cooked for him. I meet Steve for the first time and am impressed with his firm handshake and gentle, but determined face. I go over to see Bill and we joyfully exchange warm greetings.

The last time I was here I was accompanied by two friends Dan and Dina and it was early September. We'd arrived to celebrate Bill's 80th birthday at a potluck, but due to a confusion about the time, we were four hours early. Susanna was obviously irritated so I left with my companions for a hike up to Stone Face Falls. We returned and departed for home soon after, puzzled by Susanna's unpleasant welcome. A month or so later I heard that Susanna had kicked Bill out of the house the day after his birthday and I grasped the significance of her manner at last.

Now David and I sit down with Bill and after our greetings I ask what had happened. Bill tells us that the day after the party their son Jude had urged him to go to a friend's house, saying he was in danger at home. This was news to Bill, but true to his pacifist instincts he got his toothbrush and departed. He explains that Susanna, following his contraction of Parkinson's disease fifteen years earlier, had taken a lover, and suggests that the strain of supporting an invalid husband together with an indigent lover, proved too much for her and she projected her difficulties on him as the source of her problems. Be that as it may, after Bill's departure, Susanna became mentally disturbed and was hospitalized. Bill is granting her a divorce. The upshot being that he was invited back to Kingfisher Flat by the landlord, accompanied by Steve Sibley his caretaker.

"I miss her," Bill concludes, "I still love her. There's a void in me that only a woman can fill. But it reminds me of the incident of the woman who heckled George Bernard Shaw when he was giving a talk. After a vituperative exchange she concluded, 'If you were my husband I'd poison your tea!' 'Madam,' Shaw responded, 'If you were my wife I'd drink it!'" Suddenly I'm reminded of one of the most beautiful qualities about Bill: his sense of humor. Trials and tribulations come to him as to everyone but Bill survives them all by his ability to laugh.

In this interview, however, we explore the darker side of this contradiction juxtaposed with his humor. Everson's bright spirit is sourced in what critic Alan Campo calls a "gloomy" soul. This came home to me after one reading when I noticed Bill putting his poems away in his leather satchel stamped with his initials: WOE. Wiliam Oliver Everson has lived out his name in his own dialectical fashion, both in acceptance and in opposition to his name and the darkness is there in all the early poems in an indefinable way, and later in the psychological wrestlings of the years when Everson was Brother Antoninus, the Dominican.

After Bill finishes breakfast we retire to his A-frame library where he has a chair and benches set up behind his handpress. I start off by asking about his most recent minor collection of poems, *The Engendering Flood.*

•

Clifton Ross: *What do you see as the over all structure of your new epic work 'Dust Shall Be the Serpent's Food' and could you give us a preview of the next cantos in terms of what it was like to grow up in the San Joaquin as a budding young poet?*

William Everson: This series fit into the genre of the autobiographical epic, which is also called the subjective epic, a classification under which modern works like Joyce's *Ulysses* and Proust's *Remembrance Of Things Past* are included. This is my first venture into the form and it's presented problems that I solved as I went along. But that doesn't mean I've solved any to come. There's been some disruption in my affairs and I haven't been able to find my focus.

I've been reading Neruda and my fascination for him is the fact that he wrote a whole series of love poems which were essential. And you get a feeling from his work that it's basically a subjective epic. He takes the story of his life and – the main episodes, the main incidents – are his relations with women. I find his handling of it intriguing. I'd like to incorporate some of it into my own work.

My epic has presented problems. It's written in a middle style. Generally, I've written my work, *The Integral Years*, *The Residual Years* and *The Veritable Years*, in a high style, reaching for the upper register – the God register, the divine, the sacral register.

I used the epic formula in 'In Media Res', 'In the Midst of Things', which in the classic epic formula is the low point in the fortunes of the hero. The advantage of this form is that it allows the bard, the poet, in the castle hall, to encounter the audience. He starts at the most dramatic point, at "the low point in the fortunes of the hero". Then by flashback he tells how the hero got to that place. When that's worked out he narrates how he accomplishes his great goal.

I drop back in my second Canto to my father's life, using the middle style, not the high style. I worried about this. It didn't seem to me that I was writing poetry. From the point of view of what I'd been writing it seemed perilously close to prose. But my readers didn't think so. When the book was published as *The Engendering Flood*, the response of the readership was terrific. It hasn't been reviewed, but the vocal response and the epistolary response have been most gratifying and that's given me great confidence. I feel I can launch forward now.

I move from the first to the second canto which I call 'Skald'. Skald is the Norse or Scandinavian bard who sang the epics of the Scandinavian peoples. I go from there to my mother, how they (she and my father) met, how they fell in love, the problem of religion that separated them (my mother was a devout Catholic, my father agnostic). Then I told how they separated and how they found each other again. I brought it up to my own birth in Sacramento, California in 1912 and where I now await my destiny.

You asked how many cantos I plan. I don't have a plan. I don't see how I can possibly finish this epic. I'm eighty years old, going on my eighty-first year. I don't worry about that. My life is filled with uncompleted projects.

Chesterton once described a book he never wrote, which he said was by far the best book he never wrote. So in this uncompleted project – you've got a great beginning there – where does it go? What was it like to grow up a poet in the San Joaquin in the 1920s? Campo once talked about the gloom in your early poetry. Where did it come from? Did it relate to the alienation of growing up in the Valley as a poet? What was it like?

It was painful. I was hypersensitive and this hypersensitivity in itself was sufficient for alienation. I had trouble with my father. He was fifteen years older than my mother and I was clearly her favorite, which produced resentment. The problem with my father was part of the gloom. It came on before I began to write poetry as a sophomore in high school. It wasn't very good. My first early model was Kipling and that poetry had a rollicking meter, but was without substance. I went into school activities. I was a football player and made the first team. I had an accident in the final year and dropped out of football and began to play tennis. There I met my girlfriend, Edwa, who eight years later became my first wife. She was a tennis player and taught me the game. I organized a tennis club and in time became a tournament player.

I was a hunter and this took me into nature and the lure of the wilderness took me into the wild. I became what is called a "crack shot" with a 22 caliber Winchester rifle. But the problem of the meaning of life was oppressive to me.

I was raised a Christian Scientist. My mother was born and raised a Catholic and it was the Church that forbade her to marry my father. So they parted ways and she went to Los Angeles because of health problems and here she ran into the Christian Scientists. Christian Science at this time was at the height of its influence – this would be in 1905, a new century waking up. She got interested because she was in love with my father, and this gave her an opportunity. So we were all three kids raised, my older sister and younger brother and I, as Christian Scientists. But just at the time that I entered puberty my mother had her falling out with the Church elders and we stopped going. She had an over-sensitive pride and she could bear grudges. This put me on the same wavelength as my father who was agnostic. And this was the thing that impressed me.

Time went on. After high school I went to Fresno State and took a writing workshop but they didn't have sophisticated writing courses yet, just a literature course one of the faculty members taught. It didn't amount to much. I dropped out after one semester and went back home, played tennis and tried to write poetry but couldn't do it. My poems revealed more skill but they didn't have more substance.

Finally, I got a job in the C.C.C [Civilian Conservation Corps]. Roosevelt got elected in '32, took office in '33 and began his public works program which included the C.C.C. in which youth was taken off the streets and sent off into the mountains. I went in there for a year, to the Sierra, my first real taste of wilderness, living with it and growing with it. I was writing poetry but nothing of any substance. My girlfriend was going to Fresno State and she took another boyfriend. I found out about it, dropped out of the C.C.C.'s and went back to reclaim her. There, one afternoon I found a book of Robinson Jeffers on a library shelf, carried it home and read it. It was a religious conversion and an intellectual awakening all in one. I was desperate for some knowledge of the meaning of the world and the universe.

Jeffers gave me a landscape I could identify with. It wasn't a New England [Robert] Frost or a Southern poet or a Whitman in New York. It was California. The lofty Sierra range with great towering peaks... Unspeakable awesomeness. The poetry broke out of me. I hoarded it, slept with it, ate it at meals.

I dropped out and went back to the land. I was going to be the poet laureate of the San Joaquin Valley and damn near made it. I got a job working as a fruit bum in the vineyards and canneries. Edwa finished Fresno State, got a teacher's certificate, taught for a year and then we could get married. That was more common then than now. The depression was on and people were more cautious. It wasn't considered unusual to wait for a decade to save enough money for a proper place to marry and start a family.

I never had any problem about my vocation, about how I was going to earn a living. I was by instinct a manual laborer.

What effect do you think the work in the fields had on your poetry? We happen to all be from the working class and our particular class tends to be more pragmatic. For instance, we don't tend to write a poem just to make something beautiful. We usually have some intention in mind. There's a functionality about the work. Has this had an effect on your work?

Yes. The visionary. This is where the vocation is and Jung's archetypes come in.

But specifically, in terms of the fact that you had to work for a living and couldn't just sit back with an inheritance of a few hundred thousand dollars in a comfortable situation and write...

Like Jeffers. He didn't have that much money but he had enough to do it, make it be. I didn't have that. I had to work laying pipe in the vineyards in the winter and syrup-maker in the cannery in the summer, but I had a month between in the spring and a month between in the fall. Edwa worked teaching and this covered for me.

Jeffers gave me a prophetic sense. He was out to teach the world. His father was a clergyman and he rejected Christianity, but carried the Christian ethos and the prophetic strain which he got directly from the Old Testament prophets, and that witness sustained him. He admonished the world but he had the genius to body it forth in narrative poems of great power and it's in these that his great talent invested his genius. I didn't follow in this, I didn't write narrative poems. I took the shorter poems as my model and there's where I learned to write, to write profound verse. I learned to struggle until I reached a note of profundity. And this is where the gloom comes in. There's a connection between the tragic sense of life and a sense of profundity by which it is bodied forth. I was a happy guy. I didn't have anything to be gloomy about. But there was the first poem I wrote after I found Jeffers. I called it 'October Tragedy'.

OCTOBER TRAGEDY

Do not sing those old songs here tonight.
Outside, the buckeye lifts nude limbs against the moon.

Outside, the heavy-winged herons
Are scaling down into the misty reaches of the marsh.
Bitter is the wind,
And a mad dog howls among the withered elderberry on the ridge.
Bitter is the quiet singing of the cricket,
And the silent pools lie black beneath still reeds.
Go away:
Follow the spoor of a wounded buck,
Over the marsh and deep into the desolate hills.
You must never sing those old songs here again.

It's profoundly gloomy but the archetypes are there. The wounded buck. The mad dog. That's excessive but it brings a note of insanity in, the derangement of the psyche in terms of the displacement of values in the operations of life. I think I struck a note there and all the work I've done since in sixty years has been somber, profound, abrasive. It hurts. Someone said "Everson's so loud it hurts."

The life of the San Joaquin Valley went on and I would have been its prophet except for World War Two, which came and overturned that dream. My alienation shows in terms of my choice of service: I opted for conscientious objector and the draft board recorded it. I was drafted at the age of thirty, sent to the northern woods of Oregon and spent three and a half years there. And that meant the end of my marriage. The separation was too much for the relationship.

I was curious about your relation with Kenneth Rexroth. How did you feel about the editing he did on The Residual Years? *You mentioned once that Jeffers was your master and Rexroth was your mentor. Do you want to talk about that relationship?*

Jeffers was my ideal father figure, the paternal source of masculine consciousness, the element that makes us male, the attitude that constitutes our gender in a way our physicality cannot. In biology we're known to be males because of our genitalia, but that's just the beginning, setting the foundation for the synthesis and correlation of attitudinal assumptions that spell out the uniqueness that is masculine. It's a mystery. But we adhere to it. It's our identity and the source of our accomplishment.

Rexroth was more a personal father. Rexroth discovered me. Jeffers was my master, he was the archetype. Rexroth was my mentor, my coach. The coach knows what you're going to have to face, how you're going to have to maneuver, what moves you're going to have to make in terms of your career. The tragedy of my vocation is that my mentor and my master did not see eye to eye. Jeffers was not aware of Rexroth but Rexroth was very aware of Jeffers. Jeffers was a big voice on the West coast in poetry. He's never been equaled or rivaled by any western poet. He remains the archetype. Rexroth couldn't stand him and he was horrified that I should have him for my master.

What was it that Rexroth didn't like about him?

Rexroth was an experimentalist, a Modernist. Modernism is classical. It's a rebellion against nineteenth century Romanticism. Rexroth was a born Romantic but as an experimentalist he became an objectivist which is the most classical strain of Modernism. The work of art is seen as an aesthetic object. The idea was to balance it out where all the parts are together homogeneously and self supporting in a coherent system. Romantics seek transcendence. Jeffers was a transcendentalist. His great master was Emerson. He erased humanity in order to exalt the divine, the divine cosmos. Rexroth was also a marxist and a socialist and this was anathema to Jeffers. I was neither a marxist nor a socialist but I became an anarchist with Rexroth.

So Rexroth moved from marxist socialism to anarchism?

Yes.

So that was what you mentioned earlier, why Rexroth disliked Pablo Neruda, because of his supposed Stalinism.

Yes.

There's an interesting book by a man named David DeLeon called The American As Anarchist *where he shows the North American ethos as primarily anarchist. I mean marxism and socialism definitely took root in Latin America in a way they didn't here because of our national peculiarities. It's interesting that the conflict would have been embodied so in those two personalities [Rexroth and Neruda] at that point.*

Yes. That's very good. The American transcendentalist is a product of the titanic scale of the American wilderness. Rexroth understood this. His better poems, his nature poems, all celebrate this. And this is what makes him so uncomfortable with Jeffers. Jeffers did it so much better and so much more authentically because he didn't have those contradictions and complications that Rexroth had. I share Rexroth's ambiguities. I became a conscientious objector and in the camps became quite political. I encountered philosophical anarchism and became an anarchist. ...And my anarchism was a kind of pantheism. I was nearer Emerson although I never read him. I got him through Jeffers.

Rexroth stripped all of the Jeffersian influence out of my book, *The Residual Years.* Then he introduced me to James Laughlin, the publisher of New Directions, the avant garde publisher out of New York. Laughlin decided to try me out and he published a selection of my poems in the New Directions annual, the yearly collection of new writing which he uses as a trial balloon for his larger publishing arm. I'd written a pamphlet of poems when I was in conscientious objector's camp. It was called 'The Waldport Poems' after the name of the place where we were and they were about my reaction to the dislocation of my life, the loss of a woman, the loss of the companionship of a woman. And these poems are moody and sorrowful. But there's a fair amount of that in the world. Laughlin told me later they'd received more comment on those poems than anything else in the annual. And it was on the basis of this that he moved toward book production. Laughlin told me he didn't want to do a complete collection of my poems, he wanted to do a selection. I didn't have any basis for making a selection so I asked Rexroth to select for me. Rexroth went in and he cut all the Jeffers out. But that wasn't all that much. I'd written under Jeffers for five years when I was still back in the San Joaquin valley. And I'd worked out all the solutions to Jeffers' poems into my own idiom. Let me tell you something. When you encounter your master, when you fall under his aegis, you become subsumed in his presence and this is the thing that carries you through. Part of the problem with writing courses in the university today, the academic solution to the problem of writing, is the fact that, like modernism itself, it tends to stress originality. It attacks the presence of your master, does everything it can to get you to throw that off, to become original. But this is misguided. It comes about from having writing classes instead of using the apprentice method which has been world-wide the formula for the transportation of aesthetic energies from the past to the future. Something in you which is unduplicable inheres in your psyche and it speaks. You sound like Jeffers, you sound like your master... The first thing the critic tries to do is to name your influences. This puts his credentials before the reader. In it's way it brings you down to scale. You may be a sensational poet and when a critic first encounters you he works out your influences and then spills them.

David Fetcho: *That brings to mind two things. One is Collingwood, writing in* Principles Of Art, *talking about the myth of originality, saying that it's essentially a denial of human community, that we all are influenced by one another, that we all artistically take from one another, consume, eat one another's product in order to issue our own product. To hold originality as an ideal is actually a denial of the nature of our community as human beings and as artists. The other thing is what Brian Eno, the Postmodern composer, said, that there's nothing wrong with imitation because imitation is impossible and innovation is inevitable. Whenever you try to imitate you inevitably innovate. I remember a quote of yours on the poet as prophet got me to read Collingwood's book. I think it was at the end of* Earth Poetry.

Yes. Something of your own comes through in spite of your immersion in the ethos of your master. My early poems are derivative from Jeffers but they're still in print. There's enough of me in them for them to survive.

The early Mozart sounds like Haydn. The early Beethoven sounds like Mozart. The early Schubert sounds like Beethoven. And that's the way it should be. That's the continuity. Because sooner or later there comes a time when you have to speak for yourself; you face a situation that your master never had to face. And here you're forced to draw back on yourself and forget what he taught you and come to terms with it, body it forth in terms of substance.

This for me was World War Two. I had to take a stand that Jeffers didn't take. Jeffers opposed World War Two but not in terms of the same ethos that I did. I had to find a way to sustain my ethos.

Ross: *What was that ethos? I mean, what was the difference between the stand you took and the one Jeffers took?*

Jeffers thought the war was politically a mistake, that we were fishing in the decadence of Europe. We could have forced peace, he said, but instead we tended to follow Britain. We were colonials.

I took a different point of view: that life is precious in itself. The 'War Elegies' which I wrote before the camp, which were published in the camp, my poetics had changed. From a lyric naturalism I became a prophet and I spoke a rhetorical, prophetic idiom. These are not too good as poems. A couple of them stand but they don't fit very well with the Modernist ethos and they suffer from it. Those people who look for more in poetry than aesthetic objects I tend to favor.

Another thing the War did that made me different from Jeffers was it broke up my first marriage and I wrote 'Chronicle of Division', which is original work, my original work. It's a sequence in four parts on the deterioration of a relationship in great pain and it's thoroughly my own. You'd not know that Jeffers was my master. In fact, when *The Residual Years* was published – it began with 'Chronicle of Division' and went back through the 'War Elegies, Poems 1942'- Rexroth skimmed the Jeffers out of the earliest poems from San Joaquin, 'These are the Ravens' and 'The Masculine Dead', but he didn't take out any more than that. I bring the point up because none of the critics, none, none of the critics, who were constantly striving with Jeffers, took me to be an influence of Jeffers. Rexroth had done his work so well that no critic pointed at me an accusing finger.

What happened to those poems?

I restored them in the 1968 *The Residual Years* and Rexroth wrote the introduction to it.There was a critic in Madison, a strong Midwestern poet, August Derleth by name, who reviewed Jeffers and me together. Jeffers had a book called *The Double Axe*, published in 1948, which was the most repudiated book in American literature. He attacked the World War after we'd won it and he was contemptuous of the victory. And they turned on him en masse and crucified him. The critic reviewed *The Residual Years* and *The Double Axe* together and he cursed Jeffers but praised me and never once suspected the relationship between us.

Fetcho: *So Bill, how would you describe the aesthetic reconciliation in your own work between Jeffers and Rexroth's Modernism and experimentalism?*

I use it as an enhancement not as a substance. What would I use as an example of that? In 'The Tendril in the Mesh'. There's a book called *Sea Marks* by St. John Perse, a modern classic. I've never confessed this before because I wanted to keep the critics off it. I didn't want to go through all that nonsense about my influences so I never pointed to Perse as the model for that [poem]. It came out in *Man-Fate*. If you read the Perse you'd see a surrealism. (He reads 'Tendril in the Mesh':)

So the sea stands up to the shore, banging his chains,
Like a criminal beating his head on the slats of his cage,
Morosely shucking the onerous staves of his rage. And his custom
Of eyeing his plight, with malevolent fondness, never is done.
For he waits out the span of his sentence, but is undismayed;
He stands and expects, he attends
The rising up, the crest, the eventual slump of the sun.

For he bears in his groin his most precious jewel, the sacred fire of his
    crime,
Who pursued, like the beam of a laser, its solemn command,
Across the shires, red charts of his soul, the wrinkled map of his hand. And
    his heart,
Ridiculous, by someone denied, of a country preferment, never quits,
But clutches its need, like a duck. Somewhere his stain
Discolors the bride of defilement, whom rapine requested, under the form of
    his need, a ventral
Oath. But parched without peace, a swollen defeat, the cunning sleep of the
    slain.

Pluto, regnant occultist, lord of the lorns of lost space, the serene distances
    fringing the skirts of the night,
Gleaming back from his visor the farthest, most tentative beam of the light,
Whom Kore constrained, with her hesitant breast, above his rooping
    narcissist plant,
To twine in her arms his loud male thong, his truncheon desire, and the flex
    and thrill of his chant.

You asked me how the Rexrothian derivation from experimentalism and objectivism fit with the Jeffersian idiom. In that poem I brought the two together. It's more passionate than either one of them. It's more explicit. The anatomical specification is shocking. It meant to be abrasive and to rip aside the screens of convention, to level with the source of the libido. I do this by masking it in the Modernist idiom. I use an oblique reference. I counter this with the explicitness of the anatomical detail. I assume a Jeffersian transcendentalism of value and I make the voice my own. You may have noticed that St. John Perse was the master of that poem. It doesn't sound much like it as I think of it. But the fact is that when I wrote it I had just met Susanna and fallen in love with her. I'd just gone through a painful episode with the Rose of Solitude in which the attraction was sexual but in the poems it was never succumbed to. But now when I met Susanna I swept all of that aside and directly lunged for broke. The most intense poem I ever wrote. I think it's entirely original.

Fetcho: *You can even hear the tangents off in the direction of pure metaphor and magic realism of someone like Neruda in his love poetry. Not consistently throughout but occasionally through the poem you see a tangent go off in a direction like Neruda. So it's interesting now that you're coming back to look at Neruda, particularly the love poems.*

Yes. I'm wondering how I'm going to use that. I haven't yet reached a point where it's coalesced.

Ross: *Well, what I've found interesting is that, while the North American spirit has developed out of Puritanism, Anabaptism and Protestantism, Latin America has developed out of Roman Catholicism. In California you connect into Catholic America and Neruda. Or like [Ernesto] Cardenal, who mentions his two major influences being Jeffers and Pound, a similar situation with you, since Pound is a Modernist in the same vein as Rexroth. You're an American poet, but America is a mighty big continent. So discovering Neruda is coming back to that. Maybe it's just a rediscovery, coming to the same place and seeing it for the first time.*

Fetcho: *One theme that continually recurs through your interviews and discourses is the theme of the poet as prophet. I noticed in reading the transcript from the interview in 1980 you'd linked the prophetic dimension of the artist to the far-reaching universality of the redemption of Christ in the final epoch of the Spirit and I think you were using some of Berdyaev's categories in talking about that. How do you now synthesize the artist/poet as prophet in relation to the world as we find it, which is increasingly dependent on the technocratic, which is increasingly ruled by Technos, how does the prophetic confront the Technos?*

There's a movement, I don't know whether it's retrograde but there's a movement from the prophetic to the shamanistic.

In your own thinking?

Yes. I've written about it. It's in *Naked Heart*, the same interview that had the Collingwood in it. I take up the progression there from the prophet to the shaman. I didn't stress it as a confrontation with the Technos but I think it would follow that he descends to the point of disorder in the human psyche and here he meets the disorder in the psyche as a collective. He goes through his efficacious shamanizing and the deeper tensions and negative aspects of that spirit.

I think the answer lies in the liturgical. Whereas the prophet is confrontation the liturgy is reenactment. The liturgy stabilizes because it's fundamental in religion, it's fundamental in ontology, it's ontologically subsistent. Because the people depend on the presence of the shaman to keep the lines of communication clean and clear, he shamanizes in order that the tribe may be healed of its obsessions, of its sickness, its disease, its "dis-ease". That poem I just read is shamanistic. It takes that rationale and uses it in order to run it through the aesthetics. It takes the extremes of passion and physicality and sensuality to unburden the psyche in balance, obsesses the race. It corrects those, relating them on a new plane of being. Yes.

So do you think that in the emerging electronic community of the world where the development of a consensus because of instantaneous communication almost has the immediacy of a tribal context, that the poets can find a way into the performance of a liturgical/shamanistic role in order to maintain the humanity of the individuals plugged into that electronic global tribe?

Yes. That's as well as I could state it.

The problem is that those people hate poets. (Laughs) Or at least they think they do.

Ross: *Perhaps the definition of poets will have to be broadened. You were talking about the aural in Neruda. What do you see this media doing to poetry and the role of the poet?*

I think the essence is language, that the essence of poetry inheres in the universality of language. That it's this that's its guarantee of it's authenticity and it's power of assuagement and a completion of meaning, its capacity to function, to prove effective. It shows the distortion of language, the poem I read. That's why I don't fear for poetry, because of its connection to language since language is fundamental to human intellection.

THE BLOOD OF THE POET

My first remembrance: the yard of our earliest
Selma sojourn, corner of Logan
And Gaither streets, on the east side of town.

The occasion: a bevy of neighborhood children
At play on the lawn, myself among them,
And no doubt my sister, though I can't recall her.
Certainly my brother is still a mewling babe-in-arms,
Which goes far to explain the conspicuous
Absence of my mother; she is seldom without us.

Instead, a couple of neighbor women, standing by in supervision,
Complete the scene. No men around. At so early a date
In the new century, the nursery syndrome precludes it.

Suddenly the lazy summer stillness is shattered by a scream.
It is my own. I have stabbed my foot on a piece of broken bottle
Hidden in the grass. How long it has lain there,
Like a serpent coiled to strike, no one can say,
Least of all a two year old kid,
Sheltered by his mother from accidental mishap
Or archetypal malice, till the rude day dawns,
To find him unready.

      Heedless as a pup
I frolicked with my kind, ecstatic in that animal
Abasement of the self before the power of the pack,
Till the mother's untoward absence
Exposed the flaw, and in my child's
Fear-benighted reckoning the serpent
Found my foot.

      Or did my foot
Find the serpent? In the cloudy womb of causation
Who nudges whom? Falling to the ground
I twist in tenor at the seizure of my blood,
Shrieking to high heaven, bringing the scared children
And the alarmed adults crowding about me.
Someone fetches from the near back porch

A white enamelled basin, full and slopping over
With pure tap water – a household utensil
Familiar enough to the ubiquitous back porches
Of small town America; but this time it threatens.
Scrambling frantically up on my useless leg
I look wildly around for my mother. But when these sudden
Strangers seize my ankle and thrust in my foot,
I yell bloody murder.

But I quickly recover,
Brought up short by the awestruck faces
Clustered about me. I blink back my tears,
Too paralyzed by pain to see what they see,
But too rapt in the grip of the simmering archetype
Not to feel what they fear.

Then my vision fixes.
For out of my fragile, fang-pierced foot
Pulses the wellspring of my fugitive blood,
A ribbon of red, unfurling in the pellucid water,
Beautiful in its sanguinary loveliness,
Solemnly performing its surrogate office,
The changing of water to wine, as earnestly intense
As the serenade of life or the swansong of death.

Years later, under the rubric of the castration complex,
I will read it as the sleeve of a ladies favor
Tangled on his helmet where her knight lay dead,
(Slain in defense of her precious honor)
But eased by the solace of the jongleur in her bed.

So does the symbol, latent in the stuff of life,
Reconstitute its truth. But for now,
It spells only terror: this it is that fastens every eye,
Victim and lookers-on alike, in the portentous drama
Unfolding here.

So the wound bleeds on
Picking up passion as it flows, compounding its enigmatic purpose
Till that humble and hallowed icon, the basin,
That once on Golgotha caught the veritable

Gore of God, source of its numinous efficacy, only to become,
By virtue of what grave default, the World Ill's
Stinking bucket of blood?

But the ills of the world,
By God's clear injunction, are to be reckoned
Implicitly benign. His vivid signature, dazzlingly
Calligraphed on trees, rivers, rocks, buttes and benchlands,
The ordeal of life is the measure of its meaning.
Perdurably opportune, the hostages of pain
Never fail to envince the quantification of value
In the substance of the soul.

It will be roughly
Twenty more years before the tongue of this poet
Finds its true tenor. But the centrality of vision,
Which the presence of his peers, in their invincible naïveté,
Evoke within him, will, in God's good time,
Given the centrifugal passion at the heart of things,
Confirm his destiny.

Nor do I cry anymore,
But watch with amazement the limpidity of water
Undergo its savage metamorphosis,
To become before my astounded eyes,
Stunned in the existential verge of the Real,
A token of the poet's inimitable
Credentia, his consecrated blood.

Fifth Interview
The Poet and the World

Kingfisher Flat, February 5, 1993.

•

Clifton Ross: *There was a track we wanted to pursue which relates to the idea of the poet as prophet. We ended our last conversation on that subject, as you'll recall.Bill, you said in one of your interviews (*Naked Heart, *1991 University of New Mexico) that "the sensual artist and ascetic monk are largely the same, since each broaches the charismatic mode." Berdyaev and others would distinguish the two, saying "the saint orders his life as his art, the artist orders the world". Isn't it true that they relate to different energies, the saint and prophet to the spiritual energies, the artist and the poet to the erotic and creative, the body and soul?*

William Everson: Yes.

But you've pretty much equated them, haven't you? I don't know if that was just for the sake of the particular argument you were making, but would you like to elaborate on that distinction?

Yes. The theologian and the prophet deal principally with the transcendental, whereas the poet and the artist deal with the concrete under a transcendental aspect, elevating the concrete into the transcendental. But the main part remains the concrete. In poetry the reflection of the transcendental is secondary, although that might be the whole point of the poem.

David Fetcho: *In the Albert Gelpi interview back in 1976 (I think I mentioned last time we were here that this is an interview I got a lot of juice from when it appeared in a different form in* Earth Poetry.*) About the prophetic conscious-ness of the poet you say:*

"When you have become annealed in the prophetic fire, have mastered the techniques of survival in the prophetic mode, then the larger and more awesome enterprise begins to cry out to you, the wilderness within calls you deeper down.

Suddenly life grabs you and you move back and in like a crab, scuttling in protest, from the prophetic to the shamanistic. Pull down thy vanity! Retracing the historic evolution of charismatic consciousness, from artist to prophet to shaman you descend, deeper and deeper into the underblows of the race, its obscure sources of motivation, seeking to purify the murky and turbid waters of the unconscious with the electrifying kinesis of the creative act, groping for the vibration, the utterance and the Word that will crack the sleepwalker's trance of the world above you – one stroke to touch the most elemental nerve in the plasmic night out of which all life evolves, and a new age of consciousness can begin." (P.113, Naked Heart*)*

Wow!

Ross: *Yes!*

Fetcho: *Yes! Those are profoundly inspiring words. The track I want to follow on is, well, several tracks, actually. First, the source of the language, particularly of the "charismatic vocation" is one that begins with the Old Testament prophets and is rooted in the use of the word, Karis, the karismata, the gifts, the surprise, the grace, by the Apostle Paul and that has a specificity of reference in its application in the Old Testament. You've taken the archetype of the prophet and the archetype of the charismatic vocation and applied it to the development of the poet through the stages of artist to prophet to shaman. The question is almost a theological one. Did the archetype form the Old Testament prophets or did the Old Testament prophets form the archetype?*

The first one.

The archetype forms the Old Testament prophets?

Yes. The action of the prophet on the archetype is secondary. The action of the archetype is primary. That make sense?

Yes.

They're both in play. What happens is plain to see: the mode of literature decrees that the material element is going to predominate. The poet often tries to fight shy of this, striving to make an abstract statement. But he does well to stick to his last and to use his language to its full capability in its sensual dimension. You have to begin with the material and this is the essential factor that governs the process. The artist fights shy of this. He wants to be abstract. He wants to get the perfect form, the pure essence but his medium prevents this.

The question having to do with the Old Testament prophets, who introduced the concept of prophesy into our human semantic, saw their role, their stature, as a vehicle of encounter and they were obviously clear about what that encounter was with, and in transferring the prophetic function from its first specific occurrence to the realm of the archetype it sometimes seems as though the archetype forms a lateral or horizontal grid that's infinitely interesting. And yet whence cometh the archetype, what forms the archetype, what's behind the archetype? The prophets would have said Yaweh, the God of heaven and earth. What do you say in relation to the existence of the archetype and especially that point on it that is called the prophetic?

I would once have given the answer of Yaweh to that problem but I find it more complex. Now I think of it in terms of an evolving process and this evolving process is an evolution of exposure. You encounter the archetype as a horizontal grid, as you put it, but it's as if the grid is composed of several sections, each section governed by a different symbol. Take the archetype of the healer and you get all the forms of doctorhood. Each one of these is governed by a symbol and this symbol is your clue to its understanding. You sense the power but what the power is toward, you don't know. Until you relate to the symbol, and it's this that governs you in your entry into the field. With the prophet you'd have to analyze the dominant archetype of the horizontal grid, the priest and the physician. Between them lies the shaman. The shaman's health is the world ill. If I want to know what the archetype relates to in its most minute characteristic I'd come back to the problem of sickness and health. These are abstractions that can support and sustain in their complexity, a symbolic office. The prophet takes the essence of the transcendental in its simplicity...

(*The phone rings and the interview breaks off temporarily*).

•

Ross: *Where were we? Do you have your train of thought there, Bill?*

I was trying to get to the force of this question, which goes back to an abstraction like sickness or health; and the degree of materiality, ideality or transcendence that each phase registers, evokes a different vocation. You end up back where the prophet began, which is the personality. That's very fundamental and very reassuring, that you can go back to a personality instead of an abstraction or a philosophical equation. You come back to a personality, a voice saying what's right with the world. Which is why religion is superior to philosophy or psychology. If we view it in terms of personality the shaman becomes an operative intelligence who garners his force from the symbolic impact of his voice. The shaman is the healer of the ill that's troubling the tribe. He deals with the causative factor not just the individual. It's this that makes his activity a calling, a vocation: *vocare*, to be called. The meaning of all this is that you arrive at the point where philosophy ends and faith begins. And faith is simple, and warm and reassuring and very human. And it has a chastening effect on the mind. And one becomes a religious man, a worshipper.

Fetcho: *Is that how you describe yourself at this point?*

Yes. I suppose I consider myself a shaman, to go into the unconscious, grapple with the ill, the displacement and disharmony, the dis-ease. The physician deals with disease, the shaman deals with dis-ease, as the psychologist does. The psychologist studies medicine and becomes a kind of doctor. The shaman and the poet enter into the collective unconscious via the personal unconscious and engage the demon that is afflicting the spirit of the tribe. He has a profound vision of what spiritual health is and he goes into the unconscious to correct what he finds there in terms of the degrees of that health. He goes back and holds an encounter, a dialogue, which is the material element of which he is the master. You see it in the art of symbolism. The symbol is partly a sanity. This is its conscious part. Its unconscious part is an insanity: it can't be reduced to reason or to logic. He is equipped by his study of the contents of the unconscious, and by his experience in grappling with it. He takes on the character of the affliction, becomes a cripple and enacts the specific dimension which ensues. The poet does the same thing, only he projects it into a different form. But he has to have the torsion, he has to have the violence and the stress or he can't accomplish what he's called to accomplish. Most poets don't accept that risk. They make for the ideal, to create a perfect statement out of the ideal. And such impingements on the plane of reality come from them and from the nature of their form. But the archetypal poet twists his language to accommodate to the sacred character of the problem with which he's confronted.

Ross: *That's really interesting. We were talking on the way down about how in the times of social chaos there are two tendencies in human consciousness. One which is to revert back to earlier forms of social organization, and one which is to create new forms. In political terms these are thought of as reactionary and progressive tendencies, respectively. It's the institutional and the charismatic, as you've talked of it. Mussolini, for example, started out as an anarchist, a progressive, but eventually moved to fascism, "blood, soil, the fatherland". In terms of your poetry, you've considered yourself anti-modernist. How do you view your role vis a vis Modernism? You mentioned once that Modernism is based on the Newtonian view and that your own view gravitates toward the Einsteinian worldview which would indicate a progressive movement away from Modernism...*

I was Copernican by culture and affinity. That's the only way we could know, the only way we could think. But Einstein would see it differently. But they're not in communication with each other. When we're doing the work of the world and of the tribe we remain conservative. I'd be an anti-Modernist to the extent that Modernism is a last gasp of the Copernican sphere. Modernism came into being on the threshold of Einstein's discovery and is based on the affect-impacted universe. I didn't buy that world but I didn't have an Einstein to correct it. The Modernist impersonality reveals its anti-Romantic bias since Romanticism is the cult of personality and the sublime. With the death of Modernism emerges the danger of the establishment of an exceptionally conservative throwback. But I don't fear that. I've gone through that phase in my early Catholic work. I took a conservative religion and, in the teeth of Modernist aesthetic conception extolled it as something I believed to be eminently desired, that I believed in, to be cultivated and employed, not just as an alternative but as fundamental. The main thing is to keep going, to keep writing, and let the theory manifest itself in your attitude. If people want to find you post-Modernist or Neo- Romantic, let them so find you. You retain your authenticity by the directness of your apprehension. It's possible I would conceive of a poem that has a high degree of fusion between Modernism and Romanticism or Classicism and Romanticism. I think that's the best part of art today being done in the realm of poetry, the highly potent mixture of Modernism and Romanticism, Modernism and its value in Classicism, as we see it in T.S. Eliot. He announced himself a Classicist in literature, an Anglo-Catholic in religion and a Royalist in politics, for God's sake! You can't beat that! It staggers the mind.

There's Pound's fascism, his support for Mussolini with an Avant Garde poetic. This brings up for me something we talked about once. You mentioned that during Viet Nam you supported the war, something you said you later came to see as a mistake. Where's the point of departure between Brother Antoninus and William Everson and what other dramatic changes have you seen between Brother Antoninus and the William Everson of The Integral Years?

The change comes in *The Rose Of Solitude*. I finished it a profoundly different man than when I began it. I completed it just before I published *The Hazards of Holiness*, the dark night of the soul. This was the break-in-plane from the religious poetry which preceded it. In that poetry a religious idea was taken up and bodied forth in the periphery of the poem, a scope and range of associations. As I went through the love affair I endured the uprush of physical passion. I found myself back in the world of woman and out of the world of the monastic version of God and I began to adapt to the modern milieu.

This involved my shifts in regard to conflicts like Viet Nam. When Johnson escalated that war in 1964 I approved. It was no ideological change but a profound emotional one, a change in identity. In the Order I'd become an establishment man. It was the idea that the Order worked. I realized that I'd not been able to adjust to the structured world because I didn't think it could work. My problems with my father appeared hopeless and I rejected his world. His world was a world of strong nationhood, powerfully patriotic issues. It seemed to be working. I thought we could win Viet Nam hands down in six months.

I finished the Order in 1969 still convinced about the Viet Nam War and I came to teach at U.C. Santa Cruz among students who were now opposed to it. When the escalation of the war began in 1964 with Johnson, the youth of the nation responded with enthusiasm and people who'd come through World War Two were less sanguinary about it. They shook their heads at their kids but they went along with the war because they were patriots but they didn't have the enthusiasm for it that the youth showed and I didn't either. I kept real quiet about it. I traveled around from campus to campus giving my readings, avoiding the issue of the Viet Nam war and when I was forced to come out I'd support it. This went up to Watergate. And with Watergate the whole negative side of it began to invade me. It was at this point that I said I'd made a mistake. I reached the point where I accepted my previous attitude as a conscientious objector. I was never quite consistent: At the time I supported the Viet Nam War I affirmed my pacifism, up to the point of Viet Nam. It didn't make any sense at all.

You also entered the Church through the Catholic Worker movement. Interestingly enough, in 1964 probably the only people out demonstrating against the war were Catholic Workers like Dorothy Day. There was virtually no one else out there, right?

Yes.

So you were probably aware of their presence out there, right?

Yes.

How did that affect your own consciousness of them and your awareness of them.

I understood them.

Did you just think they were mistaken or duped?

I thought their position was valid. They were true to their principles, their disposition, their stance. And it was a good critique of the nationalist emphasis but it didn't change my mind. When I came to teach I found myself in hot water. It was a great relief to me to come back to my original pacifism. Viet Nam was a bad dream, bad dream in the sense that bad dreams pick up on valid elements in you and distort them into perspectives that are unacceptable to your mind. But you have to accept them, you have to acknowledge them because you've been preaching them.

Fetcho: *What kind of a dream was 'Desert Storm'?*

'Desert Storm' I was opposed to.

It's almost as though the whole nation were captured by a similar emotional impulse as you described yourself having experienced during the Viet Nam War, the same aggressive mentality that gripped the national consciousness. It became an organizing metaphor for the way that we thought about ourselves and the world. Even the name, 'Desert Storm','Desert Shield' had an almost poetic quality.

Yes.

Ross: *This reminds me of something you once said, "I don't understand it. I was against the most popular war in American history, I was for the most unpopular war." Now what you're saying about 'Desert Storm' is that you're against one of the most popular wars in the twentieth century. This makes me think of something Daniel Berrigan said, (getting back to the subject of the poet as prophet) that the prophet inevitably takes a stand against government. His view is anarchist, that government is inevitably wrong, and that it's the role and responsibility of the prophet to correct it. That's sort of what you said last time about the effect of anarchism on you when you were in the work- camp at Waldport. How does the anarchist relate to the prophet in terms of the archetype, and also in terms of your own development?*

Two questions. The archetype of the anarchist and the prophet is the same. They come from the same radical wing, reducing a process to symbolic episodes based on a vision of peace among men and love as the social adhesive that keeps society together. The second question, I've tended to live by them, I have lived by them, except for the Viet Nam period. That doesn't worry me too much. Every compromise with society represents an equation in which we hold to a part of ourselves, our conscience and our integrity. And there's a part of us that adapts on lesser issues. It's easy to be an anarchist and yet to vote for either the Republican or Democratic Party. The main issue doesn't seem to be involved. And we can do better justice to contradictory platforms. I look back on my period as a radical as one of the purest and the best of my life, just like I look back on my period of becoming a Christian as being one of the purest and best of my life. Compromise killed both of them. Not "killed them dead", as the saying goes, but subverting their imposing reality, reducing it down by compromise until it becomes a shadow of its former self. Then the war breaks out and you have to choose. You go back to the fundamental principle in yourself and choose in terms of that and hope that your biographers will have sense enough to know that you were up against a wall.

Isn't that wall also a psychological wall? I look at Gandhi, Dorothy Day and the saints of our time and think how there's something severe, one sided and almost a shadow of a person there who wouldn't reckon with the contradictions of life and make the compromises. At the same time that we admire such people we have to recognize that they have also denied an entire category of their humanity. In the compromise you made with your pantheist, anarchist pacifism by becoming a Christian and going into the Church you'd affirm that this opened a whole new area of your life in the same way that leaving the Order and reconnecting with your sexuality and elemental human realities and needs has probably opened up a whole other reality for you. I guess what I'm saying is that isn't compromise necessary in order to attain balance as a person, as a whole person?

And comprehension. Yes, that's true and very profoundly said. You try to meet the issues as they come up, one by one, each with its individual emphasis. The arguments you use on one you can't use on the other, because that's another factor of the human shortage, shortage in value, intelligence and honor. You're provoked to an extreme stance at every issue and you don't want to make an extreme stance and you want to take a balanced equation but the forces of time don't permit that. They demand that you seize a gun and start shooting. And it seems you have to choose where your gut is. I could have gone into World War Two as a medic and I would have had the consolation of maintaining my peace with my family, my friends, but I couldn't put on the uniform. I couldn't wear the insignia of the patriarchy.

As a poet I wrote my way through these various phases. I didn't tackle the Viet Nam issue head on in the poetry I was writing at that time. I hadn't gained my career emphasis as a conscientious objector and as a radical to chuck it out of hand. And I maintained that during Viet Nam. Some way or other it wasn't a very good thing to do. But I wasn't prepared to come out and assail my original World War Two commitment on the basis of Viet Nam. They just seemed to me to be so totally different. Viet Nam didn't threaten the stability of the world. World War Two did.

When I entered the Church in 1949 it was almost universal, pro-World War Two. It was completely convinced that its cause was just and this was conceived of on the basis of the atrocities that emerged with the camps surfaced only after the Nazis were defeated. The U.S. would never have gone to war to save the Jews. We went to war to preserve the balance of power in Europe and that's where it was, simply. And I found my conscientious objector stance on that basis. Fundamental. Viet Nam had no such threat as war, it was a police action. The very fact that it was not total, it had something equivocal about it.

In the poetry, it all comes out in the poetry. And my skill in making these issues into comprehensive verse. I could be a failure but I keep finding fundamental issues, fundamental stances. My sense of reality keeps changing.

I left the Order in a return to nature. I'd already found myself back there in my last years in the Order, at the time I met Susanna. When I met her I wrote 'Tendril in the Mesh', one of my most intense poems, one of my most animistic poems. It's a sequence I'm basically satisfied with. I was violating the holiest vows and yet my poetry sprang out of it, a perspective of lover's certitude. After 'Tendril' I wrote *Man-Fate* which is a period wherein Susanna and I adjusted to each other and to family life, and where I gathered up the roots of my pantheism, my animism, and discovered my persona as a mountain man to take the place of my religious habit. Trade one persona for another. This poetry is conceived on the basis of a thesis – antithesis – synthesis movement. And the justification for *The Integral Years* was that it be a true synthesis. Clif didn't think it was. And when I got here, to Kingfisher Flat, I began to move into a pure synthesis. *Man-Fate* was confessional. Confessional exacts a difficult response. It's hard to make it fundamental. But 'Tendril in the Mesh' was successful because it had passion. *Man Fate* did not have passion for its source. It had equivocation and worry, a fear of having made a mistake. But in retrospect I think this period of ambivalence was necessary and authentic.

If I'd ended at that point it would have been a loss. But I persisted through to *The Masks Of Drought*, which is the high point of the collection. When you try to see what makes them authentic it's the degree of intensity, of passion that both 'Tendril in the Mesh' and *The Masks Of Drought* touched, that gave them stability.

•

This last, brief interview took place as we worked on revisions at Kingfisher Flat, August 28 and 29, 1993

•

Clifton Ross: *What is the source of the intensity of these poems? I recall you said once (in an interview we did under the High Embrace) that you'd come to see Christ in the psychoid, that is, you'd come to know a Psychoid Christ. What did you mean by that, the Psychoid Christ? How is this different from the Cosmic Christ of Matthew Fox?*

William Everson: It was what I described in 'Dark God of Eros' (he reads the poem). The only word for that is psychoid. Jung defines psychoid as that dark, 'irrepresentable' and transcendent energy of the archetype which is incapable of reaching consciousness.

The Cosmic Christ is spatial, Its periphery is the cosmos, It's like a beam of light that stretches from one end of the cosmos to the other. It can reach from border to border of the whole creation and hold the whole scope. This is the Cosmic Christ, the full stretch. This is what Jeffers touches on when he describes the stars in 'The Loving Shepherdess':

They drew together as they drifted away no path down the wild darkness; he saw
The webs of their rays made them one tissue, their rays that were their very substance and power filled wholly
The space they were in, so that each one touched all, there was no division between them, no emptiness, and each
Changed substance with all the others and became the others. It was dreadful to see
No space between them, no cave of peace nor night of quietness no blind spot nor no deaf heart, but the tides
Of power and substance flood every cranny; no annihilation, no escape but change: it must endure itself
Forever. It has the strength to endure itself. We others, being faintly made of the dust of a grain of dust
Have been permitted to fool our patience asleep by inventing death. A poor comfort, he thought,

Yet better than none, the imaginary cavern, how we all come clamoring
To the gates of our great invention after a few years. Though a cheat, it
    works.
The speckled tissue of universes Drew into one formed and rounded light,
    and Vasquez
Worshiped the one light. One eye...
The Psychoid Christ is mad. He redeems madness in its significance. Any
insane person can understand him. We see the quintessential Psychoid Christ
in the Carrying of the Cross. He has been beaten to insensibility, functional only
instinctually, but coherent in the placement of his motor faculties. The Psychoid
Christ emerges in bed as the Bridegroom. In the marrow of the psychoid he
achieves complete coherence, unlike in the carrying of the cross where coercion
took the place of motivation. In the body of the Bride he realizes the majesty
of the psychoid. It has become his whole mode of existence. This singling out
and comprehensive realization of all that he is is his reward for fidelity to his
essential being.

The poet takes language and articulates it in such a way that the madness
is there. That's where his gonads are. He stands in a most direct approximation
to the psychoid state in his creative trance. He is utterly possessed in it. His
consciousness holds it sovereign and he comes into his own. The poems I wrote
to Susanna, 'Tendril in the Mesh', they're all mad, psychoid.

•

*Since yesterday we've gone through all of Jung's works and several other
books on theology, psychology and myth and only found passing mention of the
psychoid. It isn't even defined in the Oxford English Dictionary. Would you like
to attempt a definition here?*

I don't think a definition is in order. We can talk about it but it's more important
that we describe it than that we define it. We can locate it. There are three levels
of cognition in Thomist philosophy: The infrarational, the rational and the
supra-rational. The psychoid resides in the infrarational.

Jung, in his autobiography, Memories, Dreams and Reflections (*Vintage,
1989, p.351) says he "hazarded the postulate that the phenomenon of archetypal
configurations which are psychic events par excellence – may be founded upon
a psychic base, that is, upon an only partially psychic and possibly altogether
different form of being". He goes on to say that "for lack of empirical data I
have neither knowledge nor understanding of such forms of being, which are
commonly called spiritual. From the point of view of science, it is immaterial
what I may believe on that score, and I must accept my ignorance. But insofar
as the archetypes act upon me, they are real and actual to me, even thought I
do not know what their real nature is." [Emphasis his]*

This seems an ideal place to close the interview. Let me read the opening of my poem, Dark God of Eros'. It is the best mirror of the psychoid that I have achieved. I did not write it to illustrate that psychological dimension, but seen in the context of this discussion it seems to have realization.

Poems Of The Psychoid Christ

DARK GOD OF EROS

Dark God of Eros, Christ of the buried brood,
Stone-channeled beast of ecstasy and fire,
The angelic wisdom in the serpentine desire,
Fang hidden in the flesh's velvet hood
Riddling with delight its visionary good.

Dark God of Eros, Christ of the inching beam,
Groping toward midnight in a flinch of birth,
The mystic properties of womb and earth:
Conceived in semblance of a fiercer dream,
Scorning the instances of things that merely seem.

Torch of the sensual tinder, cry of mind,
A thirst for surcease and a pang of joy,
The power coiled beneath the spirit's cloy,
A current buckling through the sunken mind,
A dark descent inventive of a god gone blind.

The rash of childhood and the purl of youth
Batten on phantoms that once gulled the soul,
Nor contravened the glibness in the role.
But the goad of God pursues, the relentless tooth
Thrills through the bone the objurgation of its truth.

Often the senses trace that simmering sound,
As one, ear pressed to earth, detects the tone
Midway between a whisper and a moan,
That madness makes when its true mode is found,
And all its incremental chaos runs to ground.

Hoarse in the seam of granite groans the oak,
Cold in the vein of basalt whines the seed,
Indemnify the instinct in the need.
The force that stuttered till the stone awoke
Compounds its fluent power, shudders the sudden stroke.

Dark Eros of the soul, Christ of the startled flesh,
Drill through my veins and strengthen me to feed
On the red rapture of thy tongueless need.

Evince in me the tendril in the mesh,
The faultless nerve that quickens paradise afresh.

Call to me Christ, sound in my twittering blood,
Nor suffer me to scamp what I should know
Of the being's unsubduable will to grow.
Do thou invest the passion in the flood
And keep inviolate what thou created good!

THE SONG THE BODY DREAMED
IN THE SPIRIT'S MAD BEHEST

I am black but beautiful, O ye daughters of Jerusalem. Look not
upon me because I am black, because the Sun has looked upon me.
— The Song of Songs

Call Him the Lover and call me the Bride.
Lapsing upon the couch of His repose
I heard the elemental waters rise,
Divide, and close.

I heard Him tremble and I turned my head.
Behold, the pitiless fondness of His eyes;
Dark, the rapacious terror of the heart
In orgy cries.

His eyes upon me wanton into life
What has slept long and never known the surge;
Bequeath an excess spilt of the blood's delight,
And the heart's purge.

His lips have garnished fruits out of my breast
That maddens him to forage on my throat,
Moan against my dread the finite pang
Of the soul's gloat.

He is the Spirit but I am the Flesh.
Out of my body must He be reborn,
Soul from the sundered soul, Creation's gout
In the world's bourn.

Mounted between the thermals of my thighs
Hawklike He hovers surging at the sun,
And feathers me a frenzy ringed around
That deep drunk tongue.

The Seal is broken and the Blood is gushed.
He does not check but boldens in His pace.
The fierce mouth has beaked out both my eyes,
And signed my face.

His tidal strength within me shores and brunts,
The ooze of oil, the slaver of the bitch,
The bull's gore, the stallion's famished gnash,
And the snake's itch.

Grit of great rivers boasting to the sea,
Geysers in spume, islands that leveled lie,
One snow-peak agonized against the bleak
Inviolate sky.

Folding Him in the chaos of my loins
I pierce through armies tossed upon my breast,
Envelop in love's tidal dredge of faith
His huge unrest.

But drifting into depth that what might cease
May be prolonged until a night is lost,
We starve the splendor lapsing in the loins,
Curb its great cost.

Mouthless we grope for meaning in that void
That melds between us from our listening blood,
While passion throbs the chopped cacophony
of our strange good.

Proving what instinct sobs of total quest
When shapeless thunder stretches into life,
And the Spirit, bleeding, rears to overreach
The buttocks' strife.

That will be how we lose what we have gained,
The incremental rapture at the core,
Spleened of the belly's thick placental wrath,
And the seed's roar.

Born and reborn we will be groped, be clenched
On ecstasies that shudder toward crude birth,
When His great Godhead peels its stripping strength
In my red earth.

GOD GERMED IN RAW GRANITE

God germed in raw granite, source-glimpsed in stone?
Or imaged out in the black-flamed
Onyx-open line, smoldered in the tortured
Free-flow of lava, the igneous
Instant of conception? As maiden-form
Swells in the heaviness of wold, sleeps
Rumped and wanton-bulged in the boulder's
Bulk, is shaped in tree-forms everywhere
As any may see: dropped logs, say, or those crotched
Trunks pronged like a reckless nymph
Head-plunged into the earth – so Godhood
Wakes under water, shape-lurked, or grave and somber,
Where sea falls, mocks through flung foam...

                                      Ghost!
Can this be? Breather of elemental truths,
She stirs, she coaxes! Out of my heart's howk,
Out of my soul's wild wrath
I make oath! In my emptiness
These arms gall for her, bride's mouth,
Spent-breathed in laughter, or that night's
First unblushing revealment, the flexed
Probity of the flesh, the hymen-hilted troth,
We closed, we clung on it, the stroked
And clangorous rapture!

                                    I am dazed.
Is this she? Woman within!
Can this be? Do we, His images, float
Time-spun on that vaster drag
His timelessness evokes?
In the blind heart's core, when we
Well-wedded merge, by Him
Twained into one and solved there,
Are these still three? Are three
So oned, in the full-forthing
(Heart's reft, the spirit's great
Unreckonable grope, and God's
Devouring splendor in the stroke) are we –

This all, this utterness, this terrible
Total truth – indubitably He?

THE WORD

One deepness,
That mammoth inchoation,
Nothingness freighted on its term of void,
Oblivion abandoned to its selflessness,
Aching for a clue.

What clue?

Syllabled,
Shaken in its fix'd trance,
A far shuddering.

Who?

Blooms,
Subsumed in its sheer
Quality of inflection.

Endowed, the syllable
Focusing,
Determination conceives.

The concept
Borns of its pure consistency.

Not willed but perceived,
Not declared but acknowledged,
Yielded into the dimensional,
A salutation from the without.

Bearing within it strange liberties,
Consanguinations,
Dissolutions of oldness.

Rarer than the splendor it invokes,
More of wonder than its focal
Justness of perfection.

IN SAVAGE WASTES

A monk ran into a party of handmaids of the Lord on a certain journey. Seeing them he left the road and gave them a wide berth. But the Abbess said to him: If you were a perfect monk, you would not even have looked close enough to see that we were women.

— Verba Seniorum

A hermit who has lived a long time in the desert experiences great dearth of spirit, and one night, exhausted, falls asleep over his prayers. He is awakened by a knock at the door, and opening it beholds two nuns. They explain that they are on pilgrimage and have become separated from their company, and beg of him shelter for the night. he graciously shows them into his cell, and prepares to spend the night outside so that they may have its privacy to themselves. However, once inside they lock the door and throwing off their habits reveal themselves as naked succubi. They cast a spell over him, and seduce him, and there is not a shred of sensory excitation which they do not stimulate him with and gratify.

In the morning the monk wakes up and realizes he has dreamed. There is no sign of either pilgrims or succubi, nor any evidence of the disorders so real to him during the night. The monk leaves his desert cell and begins to make his way back to the world. As he goes he meets a young man, vaguely familiar to him, who is newly dressed a monk's habit and is entering the desert to become a solitary. The young monk seems to recognize him and calls him by name; kneeling before him he asks his blessing. Then he says to him: "Tell me, Father, what is the greatest blessing and the greatest curse of the spiritual life?" The monk replies: "Sleep. In sleep we dream. In dreams we betray ourselves In betrayal we discover ourselves. In self-discovery we lose our innocence. In loss of innocence we gain knowledge. In knowledge we gain wisdom. In wisdom we recover innocence. God be with you." With these words the monk leaves the young man, whom he now recognizes as himself, and re-enters the world.

I too, O God, as You very well know
Am guilty.

And the desert gorges, thos hacked
Untendered waste-worlds of the soul –
What buzzard's eye from its sun-skewered height
Has peered such places,
Pierced such deeps?

The gullies of death, the engorged

Arroyos, badlands of the hackling heart,
The scups of perversity.

I too, I too, as You very well know...

Where the kites are shrieking
There reeks the carcass.
Where the treasure is sunk
There cowers the heart.
Having done such things in the green wood
What will I do in the dry?

Guilt-stretched the night.
Choked in the abstract dimension
I see the eyes of my lust.

Have pity on me, have pity on me,
At least you my friends,
For God hath touched me.

For the light is lost.
Great darknesses drop over the waste.
The hostile stars burn green as cat's eyes
In the depth of dread.
There is not an owl on the greasewood,
There is not a saw-whet on the creosote bush
To keep a man company.

I too, O God, as You know very well know,
Am guilty.

For I sought and found not,
I searched, but was not succcesful.
When I failed, You drew back the veil,
And I am in terror.

In terror,
Who gazed in the poisonous pool.
In dread,
Who sucked of its jet.
Am sick and am sick

Who have seen to myself,
Begging forgiveness of my own self,
In what I have done.

For if You, O God, can pardon a man,
Should himself be less merciful?

Let me forgive myself of my terrible sins
That I may have peace.

Let me have mercy on myself
Or I will hang myself on a juniper tree
To wipe out my guilt.

There will be flints and grits forever in my bed.
There will be cinders in my mush.

I am burned black.
I am back from a bitter journey.
I have cruised hell.

Let me forgive myself
That thought to be a saint
And am proved a monster.
That thought to be righteous and good,
And am proved vile.
That thought myself to be the Christ
And am found the Devil.

Windless, the air dead, the night hot.
Can I find, in fact, the friendliness of a human face?

Forgive me, O God, that my heart should hold such horrors.

The vast desert stars.
The wasteless ridges.
The vacant gullies.

When I am proved out
I will come back to my people
And confess my crimes.

For I will make friends of the sinner
And comfort him in his plight.
I will pick the evildoer up from the ground
That he may take heart from his evil
And hunger the good.

I will bless the bad,
That he may be brought from madness,
May be made whole.

Speechless the stars.
No word in the wind.
The hell of nature defiled
Shuts her dread face.

For there is no man that is righteous
But carries somewhere in his salty heat
A worse villainy.

Never a man without his vices.
If any man doubts it
He has not sunk to the whoredom of his heart,
Nor tongued his own flesh.

Our loves betray us.
We give ourselves to God
And in our faithfulness
Play strumpet to the Devil.

Thus it is that my hate is scribbled about my mouth
And my lust rings my eyes.

My guilt is blistered upon my hands.
They have prized blood.
They are dabbed with sin.

O my God, my God, what can I say
Except that Thou hast touched me?

In sleep, in deep slumber,
In the raw desert night,

Thou didst send Thy holy devils
There to accost me.
As Thy terrible henchmen
They did show me me.

What visions of vastness on the moon-sunken wastes?
So dry is the night the dust-devils wander,
They whisper me out.

I will go back once more to the city of man,
Will abase myself before the sinner
For he is cleaner than I.

At least he never has claimed to be good,
Nor supposed himself righteous.

At least he does not swear by Thy truth
And live by his lies.

At least he does not bless with the one hand
While he horribly defiles with the other.

Forgive me, dear Christ, and make me as Thyself,
Who knew Thy true Self.

Hot night. The crude desert stars. The devouring distances.
There is not a coyote's howl to quaver the darkness.
There is not the scuttle of a deermouse nor the slow drag of a serpent.
There is not the mutter of a single leaf
So heavy hangs the air.

O my soul, my soul, what deaths, what pits, what savageries,
what wastes!

If I could touch so much as a piece of human dung
That some hapless wanderer dropped by a yucca
I should consider myself not friendless.

But my thoughts return upon me
And I dare not sleep,
For I am in dread of my dreams.

Therefore in the morning will I go forth
And return to the ways of man.

I will seek God henceforth in the shameful human face.
I will serve God in the wretched human act.
I will savor God in the salt of human tears.

In the body's corruptness will He be revealed to me,
In the postures of defloration,
In the deeds of wrath.

Where the murderer strangles his hope,
Where the thief plunders his heart,
Where the ogler gloats and gloats on his own self
And gloating profanes.

Out of these, out of these, will Thy peace shine forth
If I show pity.

No day? No dawn? No water? No wet?
A drop of grace for my parched tongue,
One drop would suffice me.

Forgive me, that my heart was vicious.
In my viciousness of heart
I coupled the bitch.

But in the spate of such hardness
Thou didst come to redeem me.
hadst Thou not discovered my sin to myself
Thou couldst never have touched me to forgive me.
Therefore blessed is my sin.

I will seek out a human face that I may know pity.
That I might betray and be forgiven.
That I might be betrayed and forgive.

I will seek love in the face of a man
And pity in the eyes of a woman.

I will seek faith in the brow of a child.

I will return to my mother,
To the breasts of her that nursed me,
To the lap of her that bore me.

And I will find my father.
He will bless my head.
He will forgive me.

Therefore will I be whole again,
And be made new again,
And again be made as a child.

For the night is dark.
But off in the east I see low light.
I smell the dawn.

And will find God in the thwarted love that breaks between us!

IN ALL THESE ACTS

Cleave the wood and thou shalt find Me, lift the rock and I am there!
— The Gospel According To Thomas

Dawn cried out: the brutal voice of a bird
Flattened the seaglaze. Treading that surf
Hunch-headed fishers toed small agates,
Their delicate legs, iridescent, stilting the ripples.
Suddenly the cloud closed. They heard big wind
Boom back on the cliff, crunch timber over along the ridge.
They shook up their wings, crying; terror flustered their pinions.
Then hemlock, tall, torn by the roots, went crazily down,
The staggering gyrations of splintered kindling.
Flung out of bracken, fleet mule deer bolted;
But the great elk, caught midway between two scissoring logs,
Arched belly-up and died, the snapped spine
Half torn out of his peeled back, his hind legs
Jerking that gasped convulsion, the kick of spasmed life,
Paunch plowed open, purple entrails
Disgorged from the basketwork ribs
Erupting out, splashed sideways, wrapping him,
Gouted in blood, flecked with the brittle sliver of bone.
Frenzied, the terrible head
Thrashed off its antlered fuzz in that rubble
And then fell still, the great tongue
That had bugled in rut, calling the cow-elk up from the glades,
Thrust agonized out, the maimed member
Bloodily stiff in the stone-smashed teeth...

    Far down below,
The mountain torrent, that once having started
Could never be stopped, scooped up that avalanchial wrack
And strung it along, a riddle of bubble and littered duff
Spun down its thread. At the gorged river mouth
The sea plunged violently in, gasping its potholes,
Sucked and panted, answering itself in its spume.
The river, spent at last, beating driftwood up and down
In a frenzy of capitulation, pumped out its life,
Destroying itself in the mother sea,
There where the mammoth sea-grown salmon

Lurk immemorial, roe in their hulls, about to begin.
They will beat that barbarous beauty out
On those high-stacked shallows, those headwater claims,
Back where they were born. Along that upward-racing trek
Time springs through all its loops and flanges,
The many-faced splendor and the music of the leaf,
The copulation of beasts and the watery laughter of drakes,
Too few the grave witnesses, the wakeful, vengeful beauty,
Devolving itself of its whole constraint,
Erupting as it goes.

    In all these acts
Christ crouches and seethes, pitched forward
On the crucifying stroke, juvescent, that will spring Him
Out of the germ, out of the belly of the dying buck,
Out of the father-phallus and the torn-up root.
These are the modes of His forth-showing,
His serene agonization. In the clicking teeth of otters
Over and over He dies and is born,
Shaping the weasel's jaw in His leap
And the staggering rush of the bass.

Epilogue

To confront a major addition to your aesthetic arsenal late in your creative life is an awesome event. It forces you to rethink your lifelong assumptions. You have achieved all that you had accomplished within given parameters, beyond which lay the unknown, the mystery. Then, suddenly, the darkness is pierced by a new factor. You're forced to reappraise the lifelong assumptions by which you have lived.

I must have encountered the idea of the psychoid as early as 1980, probably reading Progoff, but when preparing this manuscript for publication, Clif Ross quoted my early use of the word and I had no idea what he was talking about. Eckhardt's and Berdyaev's *Urgrund* I'd retained, but Jung's psychoid had disappeared. This did not suffice. To find Jung's commentary on the psychoid in the *CollectedWritings* is like finding the proverbial needle in the haystack. Let the reader, therefore, have recourse to Ross's introduction to acquaint himself with the field of the psychoid but here I must confine myself to the implications of this concept as it subsists in the composition of my own psychological ground.

Clif Ross has done me the honor of discovering the psychoid through the integrity of my whole subsistence to the literary core of the deep unconscious. This was not a speculative adventure. I was not an analytical psychologist but a journeyman printer and poet compelled to penetrate the area of consequence and find the root causes that were troubling man and disturbing him.

Actually I had discovered the psychoid in Jeffers. He had swept me into it and I learned the meaning of the attitude. It became my habitat, the utterness shared with all existence. The creative became my touchstone, the zone by which I centered myself in the field of existence. But, like Jeffers, I had no name for it.

When I converted to Catholicism the meaning of this development shift was to provide for the entrance of personality in the field of the psychoid. This was not a speculative venture. Rather, it indicated that I had accommodated the meaning of the unconscious, with the personality factor becoming a pressing issue. The psyche was not mature but an adolescent who had grown to the point where the intellect has become imperative and yet does not know how to engage, until, one day, quite suddenly, the intellect finds the key to its predicament and instinct, the latent factor, brings it to life. The erotic provided the theme, the track, the psychoid night provided the meat, the semen and these became my signature.

It remains only to recount that the arrival of the personality in the psychoid opened the way for the emergence of divinity, leading the way to the final stroke, the orgasm, the kiss of consummation. It brought a touch of night-plain, the nature of the soul. This is the old artist, which we call wisdom, the psychoid Christ, sure in servitude, all comprehending. I am blessed to have been shown it at the age of 81.

William Everson
Kingfisher Flat, California
March 1994